173 Pages Every College Student Must Read

173 Pages Every College Student Must Read

GETTING INTO COLLEGE IS GREAT. GETTING THE MOST OUT OF IT IS CRUCIAL.

Randy Shain

ISBN: 1543236146
ISBN 13: 9781543236149

Foreword

A wise man once taught me that, "Truth is available only to those who have the courage to question whatever they have been taught." Yet in this world of fake news and alternative facts, why are truth and courage in such short supply? Who to rely on when you discover that much of what you learned in school was either inadequate, impractical, or downright wrong? These are weighty and daunting questions I hope you consider as you contemplate what you want from college and a career.

If you feel overwhelmed or lost as you ponder the possibilities, you don't have to go it alone. Nor should you feel adrift or unprepared. There is an amazing resource out there to drown out the noise associated with college and career planning. His name is Randy Shain, and he proves convincingly in this book that the number of un...and under-employed college graduates prove that sailing solo is ineffective. In a world that values specialization, the need for a trusted guide, advisor, and support professional to help navigate these murky waters is vital.

Given the enormous financial investment in yourself, expectations for an undergraduate degree are no longer "graduate from college and a great job awaits." To presume a reasonable return on your investment should be the norm as the stakes are too high to leave to chance. Randy convincingly asserts that education should not be narrowly dedicated to expanding minds and learning to think critically. In this highly competitive world with prime jobs so scarce, if you pay a small fortune for your education, you should expect an exceptional outcome when that diploma is finally granted.

Nevertheless, as Randy so eloquently stresses, "Learning WHO to ask for help, learning HOW to ask for help, and learning to integrate that help into ACTION are skills that benefit us all." Where then do parents, high school, and college students turn to for straight talk, practicality, and actionable advice? The answer lies within the pages of this engaging and powerful book.

I had the pleasure of meeting Randy through a mutual friend named Lori Ann Bassil. She sent me an email out of the blue communicating, "You should meet him. I think the two of you will hit it off." At the time, I had left a twenty-five-year Wall Street career to dedicate my next chapter to teaching college and coaching corporate leaders. I came to happily learn that Randy was also in his own career transition. When he described the goal to form One on One mentors on the heels of a thriving career as a business owner, it made perfect sense.

Page after page of this superb book, I kept shaking my head in agreement, elated, though not surprised, that Randy wrote this with such convincing insight. Through most of it I wondered, "Why didn't anyone tell me this when I was in college?" It starts with helping you develop the proper mindset before you even consider the skills that should follow. More important, he puts in perspective the all-too-common scenario of what to do post-graduation if you find yourself broke, helpless, and without a solid first job. The good news, as you'll soon discover, is that this can be prevented.

I'm thrilled that Randy is striking a resonant chord. The book is chock full of research, anecdotes, and stories that underscore the importance of getting this foundation of your life just right. It provides sound advice from an experienced and passionate authority. He even communicates that, God forbid, it's ok to fail. But, that doesn't excuse you from walking around aimlessly without a plan. You'll learn to sort through the confusion as he brings clarity to the sheer quantity of mixed messages you're likely to hear. He also guides you through the tools and techniques needed for an actionable career blueprint.

Randy also makes a compelling case why you need a mentor. As a student in your transition to become an adult, it can be puzzling to find the right equilibrium of "do it yourself" with having the courage to ask for help. His indispensable advice, including a homework assignment after each chapter, is the ideal prescription to cure the college ills that cause so much unproductive anxiety.

Even better, his cleverly organized chapters are a series of encouraging action items meant to inspire you to uncover the tactics to invest mightily in your future self. You will not learn this in high school, and the career counseling departments in colleges are understaffed, overworked, and lack the requisite experience to provide the value you deserve. Hence, there is a vibrant and masterful alternative. Randy's strong message that you need a mentor along the way is compelling. You've invested too much time and money to have to figure it out yourself.

Thus, you're not alone. You have an exemplary One on One mentor. I'm proud to call Randy my friend, and he has an open door to any class I teach. Written in straight talk with his keen sense of humor, this book is much more than a "How to" and "Call to Action." It's a bible to be read in high school as you envision your college prospects. And, like THE bible, it's meant to be re-read in college, and again in your transition to adulthood.

Finally, as I finished the book, I was reminded of John Keating, the character played by Robin Williams in the movie *Dead Poet's Society*. Keating was an inspiring teacher, had the courage to defy convention, and urged his students to "strive to find your own voice, because the longer you wait to begin, the less likely you are to find it all." I see some of myself in that character. And I see a lot of Randy in him as well. Maybe that's why we get along so well. He brings the courage and conviction to say what needs to be said, and zealously advises you to do what needs to be done.

In your quest to speak up and strive for success, what a privilege to have Randy with you on this wonderful journey. As you read the book, you'll come to know a successful, passionate, and deeply committed professional dedicating his time and expertise to help you to help yourself. In this process of self-discovery, he'll provide the necessary assistance to underscore that life is not just about finding yourself, it's about creating yourself.

It takes your commitment, an open mind, and the desire to listen to a respected guide to climb that mountain of success. While Randy will teach you to cut through the clutter, he'll bring the right mix of empathy, compassion, and tough love. Don't be surprised on your journey if he reminds you of what Winston Churchill said many years ago, "Success is not final. Failure is not fatal. It is the courage to continue that counts."

Thanks Randy, for bringing your wonderful work to a larger stage. I'm grateful for your friendship and proud to be a partner in your mission to make a difference in the lives of others.

Chuck Garcia
CEO, Climb Leadership International
Professor of Organizational Leadership, Mercy College School of Business
Author of Amazon Best Selling Book *A CLIMB TO THE TOP: Leadership & Communication Tactics to Take Your Career to New Heights*

CHAPTER 1

Introduction

Most of the advice we hear and read seems like it was designed for a seven year-old. How often do we hear a basketball coach telling a kid that the team simply needs to score more, or a teacher asserting that a student needs to focus? These are worthy goals; how to reach these goals, sadly, is rarely discussed.

This book will do the opposite. Much of what is written here is designed to help college students (principally those focused on the liberal arts/humanities) learn *how to* make the most of their four (or more) years of undergraduate education. If I do my job, every reader will learn how to determine what they *really like to do*, what they're *good at doing*, and how those two things translate to a job they *want to do*.

The business I founded interviewed thousands of recent college graduates over a two decade period. We hired hundreds of them. Many are still there. I trained a great number of them, and had the privilege of watching them develop into managers running their own departments. This experience taught me many things about organizational behavior and motivational tactics. I made tons of mistakes, each of which taught me how to be a better businessman, and more importantly, a better person. I understand deeply the kinds of actions and attitudes that employers look for in their employees. I am confident that I can impart these lessons on the young people who take the time to read this book.

During the last few years, I have extended the informal mentoring role I played at my former company to students still in college. Through my new firm, One on One Mentors, LLC, I am deriving intensely gratifying emotional rewards helping students achieve what they believed to be out of reach. Each time I discuss this with people, the response is almost always a variation of this: "I wish someone had done this for me in college. Then I wouldn't have wasted 5, 10, 15 years figuring out what I wanted to do with myself." If I accomplish anything with this book, it will be to prevent even one kid from uttering that distressing sentence.

Talk to college students about the future and invariably you'll get one of the following three responses:

1. I'm lost. I have no idea what I want to do when I graduate.

2. Everyone tells me to find my passion. How am I supposed to do that?

3. I know what I want to do, but I don't know how to make it happen.

Talk to parents of kids in college, and this is what you'll hear:

1. I'm paying a small fortune for college, so they must be guiding my kid into a career path.
2. My kid just needs to figure this out for himself, like I did.
3. It doesn't matter if they like what they do, as long as they get a job when they graduate.

Let's examine each of these assertions individually.

Things Students Say

I'm lost. I have no idea what I want to do when I graduate.

This is by far the most common sentiment voiced by students I know. It's at once depressing and completely understandable.

Why would adults expect teenagers to know precisely what job suits them best? This is especially true of college freshmen; the most vivid description I've heard about this was from a new college student who asserted, "You want me to decide on my life when a few weeks ago I had to ask permission to go to the bathroom?"

Most college students simply don't have the job and even life experience to know what career paths might fit them. In and of itself, this is not a problem. College is a four-year learning process where young adults can discover and work on their skills and interests, without having to earn a living. Obviously, the issue arises when at graduation, you realize you have no more of an understanding of what you want to do than when you started.

Why does this happen so frequently? The word "lost" is the best clue. I am the type of person who can get lost traveling to a place I've been to 500 times, while using a map and listening to the GPS directions. The only way for me to avoid this is extra planning; I resort to writing down directions I've transcribed from Mapquest onto a piece of paper. It's a little more effort, but for me, the payoff is well worth it.

Now imagine if I were trying to reach an unknown destination. For many college students, even the ones who unlike me are not "directionally challenged" (i.e., with an embarrassingly low spatial sense), figuring out where to go without any plan is nerve-wracking and too often, ineffective. Many students never figure it out. More than half of 2014/2015 graduates surveyed [1] in 2016, in fact, "considered themselves to be underemployed. ..."

This book will teach you how to map out your future, one where you feel content in your job, instead of dreaming of being somewhere else.

---

1 https://www.accenture.com/t20160512T073844__w__/us-en/_acnmedia/PDF-18/Accenture-Strategy-2016-Grad-Research-Comparison-Infographic-v2.pdf

Everyone tells me to find my passion. How am I supposed to do that?

Good question. When I explain to people that trial and error is actually effective, I'm occasionally met by a look that's normally present only after seeing a UFO, or the Jets winning the Super Bowl (an even less likely occurrence). Practical learning, or simply learning by doing, works. It's not magical. It will lead to some frustration, and maybe some tears. But it works. (And yes, some people will have a relatively short timeline for this to occur, depending on financial circumstances, say. This is why starting the process at the onset of college is so important.)

Part of the trial and error process involves asking for help. Before you even begin to explore different interests, you'll at times be forced to ask a grown-up for advice as to how to start. And this is where I sense the first stumbling block exists. Many students despise and/or fear the very thought of asking anyone for anything – in person. Going online to make a reservation? Piece of cake. But calling to make an appointment? No way. Not going to happen. Better to find another vendor with a web-based solution to avoid the hassle of personal interaction. The problem with this method is that at college and in the job world, most of the people you'll interact with are older. They are used to dealing with questions in person. They want to continue this mode of communication. For you to get where you need to go, you'll have to get used to this. Unnatural, yes, but critical.

I also fully recognize that many teenagers feel nothing but stress when told that you are supposed to have fully developed work passions. In part, this is why I devote a whole chapter to this process (Chapter 7). For now, recognize that being surprised that you don't know what you'd love to do for a living is like never having seen an ocean and being surprised that you can't surf.

Assume that after reading this book you learn how to find what appeals to you most. The next question is why this matters. Clearly it's better to work at something you enjoy and not something you hate. Still, I'm sure you've heard some variation of this phrase, "It's called work for a reason." But does work have to suck? According to a 2014 Gallup-Purdue Index,[2] which included interviews with more than 30,000 U.S. graduates, "where graduates went to college — public or private, small or large, very selective or not selective — hardly matters at all to their current well-being and their work lives in comparison to their experiences in college. ... If an employed U.S. college graduate recalls having a professor who cared about them as a person, one who made them excited about learning, *and* having a mentor who encouraged them to pursue

---

2 http://www.gallup.com/poll/168848/life-college-matters-life-college.aspx

their dreams, **that graduate's odds of being engaged at work more than double** (bolding added for emphasis). Yet, only 14% of college graduates strongly agree that they had support in all three of those areas."

Chapter 9 deals with how you can form relationships with professors. In Chapter 11, you'll learn how to find the right mentors. The combination will spur you to find the things that excite you by trying many things, many times. Making good money while being miserable at work isn't a goal. Be one of the 14%.

I know what I want to do but I don't know how to make it happen.

The focus of this book is on students who are not pursuing highly specific paths. Pre-med, engineering, accounting and even some finance majors might see this book as superfluous. That's OK. But even people with a highly-defined career path are often completely unclear as to how to achieve this goal.

Acknowledging this, I've devoted multiple chapters to so-called hard skills. Chapter 10 describes how to build a network. In Chapter 12, you'll read all about internships, from how to secure them to what types might be right for you. Chapter 13 delves into résumés and cover letters (fun stuff); Chapter 14 teaches you how to take the nervousness out of the interview process. Finally, in Chapter 15, the grand finale: how to take all of this information and use it to secure a job that you want.

Things Parents of College Students Say

I'm paying a small fortune for college, so they must be guiding my kid into a career path.

Many colleges actively pretend they are guiding your job path, when they simply cannot possibly do so due to the numbers. Colleges are being challenged to produce a return on investment (the dreaded ROI). Rather than explain what they actually do, many feint, sadly. I recently spoke to a school with 17,000+ students. The school advised that it has a program designed to help students determine their best job path, based on their interest and skills. Sounds great until I learned that fewer than 20 counselors exist for the entire school; at a 1 counselor to 850 student ratio, it's clear that few if any students could possibly receive the personalized attention they require to make such an important discovery.

No matter how well intentioned, I've been told that it's often difficult for these counselors even to promptly respond to emails, much less have a regular dialogue with students. Moreover, as one student at an elite university put it to me, how can his overloaded career counselor, who has not worked outside academia in decades, advise him on a world in which he hasn't participated? While counselors undoubtedly care about their students' success, no one cares nearly as much about an individual student's success than that student.

The above ratio is not at all unusual. Career services departments primarily help with résumés and steer students to career fairs or the college's internal job board. This is fine for the relatively few students pursuing consulting, finance or accounting. For the rest of you, good luck.

College career services offices often function the way large high school guidance counseling offices do. It's not necessarily the college's fault; to employ the type of staff required to provide one on one coaching would be extraordinarily expensive. The crucial point here is for parents to understand the limitations of these offices, and to act accordingly.

Sometimes students receive an even more insidious message. Multiple students majoring in business have expressed their frustration to me about being consistently pushed into accounting or finance, even after explaining to teachers and administrators that they like neither. From a college's perspective, what is most important is that when students leave, they have a job. Students finding jobs they want is a far lower priority.

Mentoring also gets short shrift at most colleges. You'll occasionally be told in your tour of a school that students can access peer mentors, or professors, or the network of alumni who have volunteered to serve in this role. Stripped of the niceties, however, this amounts to very little, mostly because the people cited here simply do not have the amount of time it takes to be truly effective in a mentoring role. Certainly there's a role for this type of auxiliary mentoring, but to believe that a typical student will gain self-knowledge from this system is a huge stretch.

A young man I mentor is incredibly driven to achieve his goal of building a thriving real estate investment company. Only 24, he is well on his way. When I asked him about his college experience, he responded that he developed his passion entirely on his own. He added, "College doesn't teach students how to discover their innate skills and how to apply those skills to a field of interest in a long-term, sustainable way. Colleges also don't teach the persistence and character that is necessary to pursue the key players and gatekeepers of whatever field ultimately is selected." This book will help you achieve all of these things.

In Chapter 11, I'll discuss the incredible benefits mentors play for the few college students, sadly, who take advantage of this opportunity. Like Obi Wan to Luke Skywalker, or Alfred to Batman, the hero always has a mentor and it's almost never a parent (most parents know that our kids would rather listen to advice from the UPS man than from us, even if we really are job-finding experts, which most of us are not).

I've discussed this at length with a very thoughtful friend of mine, Matt Harris. According to a January 30, 2015 story in the *Washington Post*, **four out of five students graduate college without a job.** [3] Matt's take on this article is as follows:

> The article suggests better efforts at getting businesses to recruit. I don't think that's where the solution is going to come from. The solution is changing kids' mindsets, lighting a fire in them, giving them the skills and support they need to realize their full potential.
>
> What are the most successful movies at the box office? Heroes' journeys. There's a deep human need to discover and fulfill our greater human potential. We need to foster the next generation to discover their own origin stories. ....
>
> What do you think of when I say mentor? Me? I think of a whiny teenager cleaning robots on a dusty farm on Tatooine who learns to use the force. I think of a bullied new kid in town getting his ass kicked day after day, who learns the power of the secret Crane kick. When I think mentor, I think Obi-Wan Kenobi, and Mr. Miyagi, and this may make you chuckle, but that's the impact you want to make on the life of every student you take on. To set them on the path of being their fullest, most incredible selves. That's the hero's journey at One on One.

What if we focused less on guidance, and tasked colleges only with career preparation. According to a recent Gallup poll, only 14% of Americans say they "strongly agree" that college graduates are well-prepared for success in the workplace. [4] "And business leaders are even more skeptical, with only 11% saying that college graduates are

---

3 https://www.washingtonpost.com/news/grade-point/wp/2015/01/30/more-than-4-out-of-5-students-graduate-without-a-job-how-could-colleges-change-that/?utm_term=.c1fa0867aa47

4 http://www.gallup.com/topic/blog_tgb.aspx

well-prepared for success at work." Astonishingly, "96% of chief academic officers of colleges and universities are either somewhat or very confident that they are preparing college students for success in the workplace."[5] I'll grant that college academics are being honest with their answers. Sadly, though, I don't think their opinion counts. If businesses question students' preparedness, it's not up to us to tell them they're wrong. Rather, we'd all be better served helping students close this incredible gap.

My kid just needs to figure this out for himself, like I did.

This is a bunch of hooey. Here's a quick poll: how many people reading this are still doing the same job (even if you've switched companies) since college? More to the point, how many of you feel fulfilled by that job?

From people with whom I've spoken, those answering yes to both questions is very low.

Let's all think about that the next time we tell a college kid they should "just figure things out on their own, like we did." The instinct to allow our kids to learn from their failures is certainly admirable. Conflating this with wanting them to learn everything on their own isn't. Even if this generation was as plucky as their parents, learning this way is incredibly inefficient. A primary benefit of forming relationships with older students, professors and other adults is learning from their mistakes. Hearing about others' blunders won't make you mishap-free. But gleaning nothing from others is far worse.

Kids of this generation also face some unique pressures:

1. Competition

   According to one estimate,[6] more than 20 million students are expected to attend American colleges and universities in 2016, 5 million more than did just 16 years ago. This rise is owed both to an increase in the traditional college-age population as well as a rise in the percentage of students enrolling in college. 1.9 million students are expected to earn a bachelor's degree in 2016. Less than half[7] that many earned a bachelor's in 1987.

---

5 http://www.gallup.com/businessjournal/174275/education-economy-america-next-big-thing.aspx

6 https://nces.ed.gov/fastfacts/display.asp?id=372

7 https://www.statista.com/statistics/185157/number-of-bachelor-degrees-by-gender-since-1950/

2. Facebook Fishbowl Effect

    The Facebook Fishbowl Effect can be defined as follows: proximity leads to comparisons, which in turn lead to feelings of inferiority. Facebook exacerbates this. When was the last time someone posted that they failed a test, got rejected by a prospective employer, got dumped by a boyfriend or missed the free throw that would have won the game? An alien looking at Facebook for the first time would conclude that everyone on the planet is doing amazingly well. The outgrowth is those having problems believe they are the only ones doing poorly. The realities, of course, are that every new college student faces challenges, and few have all the answers immediately. Social media, sadly, reinforces a false narrative that can lead to real problems.

    A big state school sophomore I mentor explained to me that he was afraid he'd be getting behind if by the summer before his junior year he didn't have a "good" internship, like his friends had been getting. He completely overlooked all that he'd accomplished already. He didn't recognize that if these other internships were terrible, which many undoubtedly would be, their value would be questionable (we'll go over this at length in Chapter 12). Finally, he couldn't conceive of how a summer with a grunt job combined with volunteering could deliver both immediate and long-term rewards. All he could see was that his friends had name-brand internships.

3. Enormous Cost of Failure

    Let's face it: college is friggin' expensive. A four-year private college education is running in the $300,000 range, or about twice what I paid for a huge house a few years ago (OK, it was more than a few, but you get the idea). Combine this price tag with the increased difficulty in finding full-time jobs post-graduation, and you get nothing but stress. Walking out of college and being unemployable is not an option, but too often it is a reality.

4. Parental (Over) Involvement

    In Chapter 2, we'll review some effective strategies and tactics for preparing our offspring for college. We'll also examine some tactics that are awful. For now, let's simply accept the fact that parents of today are FAR more involved in our kids' lives than our parents were in ours. Before entering college, I delivered newspapers (back-breaking), been a lifeguard (foot warts, thanks), worked at Burger King (gross), and scooped ice cream (snooze), among other jobs. Not once can I recall my parents driving me to any of these jobs. Nope, I walked, or rode my bike. My parents didn't know my work schedule. They didn't come watch me play sports. They rarely helped me with homework, and didn't know where I was. Sure, I was expected to be home at a certain time, but beyond that, they were not concerned. My parents missed out on a lot of my comings and goings, owing both to their work schedules as well as to societal norms.

Does any of that sound like the way the typical parent acts today? I deliberately worked most of the time from home so I could be there after school. I loved it. And like any parent, I hate seeing my kids hurt. Being around all the time and instinctively looking to protect them can lead to stepping in and fixing things for them. This isn't helpful; it's crippling, and according to numerous psychologists and kids, has led to an enormous uptick in anxieties and depression. Too often, kids of today have been told what to do, handled and pampered, leaving them unprepared to handle rejection and failure, hallmarks of the "real world."

5. New Economic Conditions

The information economy is very different than the industrial economy we had as kids (hats off to my friend Joe Maissel for this insight). In a story examining the differences between modern and industrial age[8] classroom settings, a section entitled "Needs of the Economy" caught my attention. The Industrial Age description of what companies needed from workers was this: "Ability to 'fit in,' follow orders (chain of command), think inside the box, perform as directed; expectation that tasks/assignments would not vary much in one job description." Information Age employees, conversely, are expected to place a "higher priority on networking, people skills, communication skills, creative thinking ("outside the box") and problem solving, initiative, flexibility, adaptability; ability to multi-task, shift gears, change to shifting demands of the workplace; people with "vision and attitude."

---

8 http://www.educationworld.com/sites/default/files/bluestein-industrial-vs-information-age-revised.pdf

Flexibility sounds appealing on the surface, but to many students, having to adapt, network and be creative all the time is actually intimidating, not liberating.

So where is all this pressure and stress going? According to a number of news[9] stories[10] quoting mental health studies, students are "buckling" under the strain they feel. Ill-prepared to manage stress or even tolerate discomfort, yet having more of both even upon entering college, is an extremely problematic combination for students. "More than half of students visiting campus clinics cite anxiety as a health concern,[11] according to a recent study of more than 100,000 students nationwide by the Center for Collegiate Mental Health at Penn State." And "nearly one in six college students has been diagnosed with or treated for anxiety within the last 12 months, according to the annual national survey by the American College Health Association."

Before you exclaim that the above factors are just an excuse for kids' flops, let me assure you that this book is designed to coach, not to coddle. Readers will work harder than their peers; students will discover how to foster their passions; how to advocate appropriately; how to present themselves to employers; and how to act while on a job. No one can do this for them, but nor can they do it without input. This book is about helping them see the greatness in themselves. Once that happens, worries about their futures will dissipate.

It doesn't matter if my son/daughter likes what he/she does, as long as he/she gets a job after graduation.

Ugh. The appeal of safety and security is palpable. Fulfillment, contentment, thriving – these are just words. Concepts. But not reality.

If I accomplish just one thing with this book, I pray it's relegating this terrible theory to the junkyard of bad ideas.

Working at large companies with recognizable names is perfectly fine ....for kids who are genuinely interested in doing so. For kids who aren't, "guiding" them on this path is taking care of their immediate financial needs and putting parents' fears to rest. In doing so, however, a far larger issue is created: kids are miserable. What's more, this deep dissatisfaction with work is difficult to fix, especially as time marches on,

---

9 https://well.blogs.nytimes.com/2015/05/27/anxious-students-strain-college-mental-health-centers/?_r=1
10 https://www.nytimes.com/times-insider/2015/05/28/anxiety-on-campus-reporters-notebook/
11 http://ccmh.psu.edu/publications/

paychecks are cashed, bills accumulate and responsibilities accrue. Avoiding this folly upfront is far easier than unlocking the golden handcuffs later.

Getting any job is not a goal. Getting a job you might want – that's something to target.

This article [12]beautifully encapsulates this theme. And if this section doesn't give you shivers, I'm not sure what would:

> "My job at the law firm was the first that my ambitious parents — both first-generation college graduates — had ever been truly proud to hear about. It was also, by far, the worst I'd ever had."

Taking a job to please other people almost never works, in the long run. Use your time in college to figure out what you love, and how to translate THAT into something you do for money (as long as it's legal).

Self-discovery comes with the college journey. Unfortunately, a huge void exists between understanding yourself and figuring out how to apply that to a job within a field of interest. To complicate things, the adult work environment is drastically different from that of college. Many students struggle to make the adjustment, even in the unlikely event that they have stumbled their way into a reasonably satisfying job. If I do my job, this book will teach students to both recognize their greatest strengths and the things that truly mesmerize them, as well as how to take those things into the workforce.

Ok, you've probably had enough of the metaphors. Practically, this book will take students from freshman year in college, through graduation and beyond. Readers will learn how to:

- Prepare for college.
- Set goals (bucket lists) and make plans to reach those goals.
- Select classes by uncovering your real interests, not those of your parents or peers.
- Write; speak in public; work in teams and think critically.
- Pick a major based on those interests, combined with the school's offerings.
- Develop passions through trial and error.
- Discover the balance between school, extra-curricular, work and social activities.

---

12 https://www.nytimes.com/2016/01/03/jobs/a-job-that-nourishes-the-soul-if-not-the-wallet.html?_r=1

- Foster lasting relationships with professors.
- Build meaningful networks.
- Identify and work with mentors.
- Uncover appealing jobs and career paths.
- Navigate the summer job/internship process.
- Write effective résumés and cover letters.
- Hone interview skills.
- Accelerate your job readiness process.
- Understand how to behave while at work, how to deal with a boss, and how to make yourself indispensable.

One last indulgence before I get into the nitty gritty. The incredible Frank Bruni recently spoke at my local theater, the Landmark on Main Street, as his book, Where You Go is Not Who You'll Be,[13] just came out in paperback.

He started with a story that I think summed up a good portion of his speech, his book, and the mantra of One on One Mentors. He was asked to teach a class on writing at Princeton University. He could only accept 16 students but received 48 applications. After reading them all, he couldn't pick between them, given their high quality, so he simply chose at random. Midway through the semester, he noticed the actual work assignments for more than half the kids never again approached what he had liked so much in their applications. He asked a number of faculty members about this, with all expressing no surprise at this outcome. Their takeaway? Kids are being taught that the idea is to be great at getting into things – so they prioritize that – and that it is not so important what happens afterwards.

We at One on One Mentors have one goal: to change this backwards view of how success is attained. Too many kids are needlessly failing to reach their potential. Too many graduates are miserable at work, years after they left college. This should not be an acceptable outcome. I believe young people today can be truly remarkable, with steady guidance and an occasional push. I hope to influence some of you with this book.

And I hope you'll remember that getting into college is great. Getting the most out of it is crucial. Tm

---

13 https://www.amazon.com/Where-You-Not-Who-Youll/dp/1455532703

CHAPTER 2

Parents Preparing Kids for College

What can parents start doing to help prepare their high school seniors for leaving the nest? As a parent of a college junior and a high school senior, and as a founder of a company that specializes in working with college students, I often am asked what parents can do to prepare our soon-to-be collegians (and college freshmen, truth be told) for life away from home.

Rather than just draw on my own experiences, I thought it would be productive to hear from some college kids, all of whom just went through this experience and moreover, are the ones who actually see the results.

The following highlights what I have learned so far; each year I'm sure there'll be more.

Treat Your "Kids" Like Soon-to-Be Adults

Of course an 18 year-old isn't really an adult, and we've all read how the brain doesn't fully mature until years later. Still, there's no better time than now to treat your high school senior like an adult, especially considering that in only a few months he'll be off basically on his own. Some specific steps to take here include the following:

1. Adjust Curfew

   Counter-intuitively, my parents basically eliminated my curfew prior to my senior year; before this, I had the tightest curfew of anyone I knew. Their reasoning was simple: I might as well learn, while they could still help me, rather than make all my mistakes with no adult around. You don't have to be this radical, but there's no question that pretty soon your kids will be up until all hours of the night/morning, so worrying about when they come home now might not be best for either of you. (Here I'd caution that I am still a believer in having some curfew, just not an early one. More important to me is the idea that we will always wake up to drive anyone home who is unable to get themselves home.)

2.   Listen, Don't Judge

Most parents I know would rather bite a rusty piece of sheet metal than bite their tongue. Remaining silent while observing our kids making mistakes seems unnatural, at best. Worse, though, is judging their decisions. Listening, meanwhile, helps foster a relationship where kids will reach out when they do need advice, rather than hiding their problems from you. Don't make them liars; if you ask a question that they answer truthfully, stay calm and work through a plan for the next time. As one of my son's friends expressed so beautifully, "Starting college is a tough time, and it's even harder if you can't confide (at least somewhat) in your parents."

3.   Ask Before Nagging

My good friend Robin Sigman taught me a wonderful lesson about "following up," i.e. nagging. Robin believes in having a real discussion with your kid to determine whether they wanted reminders about any topics, and if so, which ones, instead of just being on top of them constantly. Some kids may actually not mind being told what to do all the time; even so, soon enough you won't be there to serve that role, and they may be unprepared to fend for themselves as a result. More likely, your kid may want reminders about certain things (say, to practice driving in advance of a driving test) but ask for freedom to study, practice sports and find summer work on his own. It's admittedly quite difficult to follow through on this, and you may have mis-steps. Still, once you get in the groove, you may find that you feel both less stressed and proud that your teenager actually handles things very well without your "help."

An amazing basketball coach I know is fond of saying that your preparation needs to match your aspirations. What I've taken from this is that the "your" in the sentence is the key; the coach is referring to the kids, not the parents. If your kids have goals they want to reach, then they need to plan and prepare to meet those goals. If they fall short, so be it. But it's extremely counter-productive for kids to prepare to meet goals that are really more of what their parents want. Obviously, there's a spectrum here, and you'll have to gauge whether you're OK with your kids doing things in a way that differs from the way you'd do them. Once again, though, remember that in a few short months, there will be very little you can do to control what they do.

Another wonderfully insightful friend Paula Whitman (whose business specializes in helping students with their college essays and applications[14]) summed this up by explaining that we parents have to find ways to realize that our kids' failures are not ours (just as their successes belong to them too).

Be Patient

Many high school seniors are incredibly moody the summer before college, often because they are scared and sad about leaving home. Be aware of this, and as hard as it sounds, don't take it personally when they act oddly, or even when they are nasty. Easier said than done, but just remember you're not alone in wanting to pour a pitcher of water over your kid's head from time to time.

Routines

One of the most common trepidations for incoming freshmen involves time management. College isn't like high school where a student comes home, has a snack, then sits and does homework. Some days they'll have one class, whereas others they'll have none or five. Having an everyday routine and planning ahead is critical; it is imperative for parents to discuss this with their rising college freshmen. I'd take this one step further and advise using an online calendar like Ical, Google Calendar or Outlook, and/or the old-fashioned monthly planner you buy at Staples.

One way of ensuring a smoother transition is not structuring your senior's free time as much as you had in the past. Suggest activities, sports, clubs, and such, but don't force it. Many students come to college without having learned how to manage their free time and end up partying too much or binge-watching Netflix. Better they

---

14 http://www.pwessays.com/

should learn how to balance their time commitments while under your roof, not after they get a 1.8 GPA first semester while being able to recite Narcos' episodes verbatim.

Teach Them the Basics

Growing up with two working parents meant learning to cook, clean and do laundry before even entering my teen years. Naturally, I failed to impart this lesson on my own kids, who have had to learn it on the fly while in school. A far better method is showing them basic stuff, from how to fry an egg and how to cook pasta to how to turn on a washing machine, before they head off. It's not that difficult, and yet it's incredibly empowering.

Speaking of Basic, Buy an Alarm Clock

Kids go to bed late, and thus have a hard time getting up early. I'd argue that high school should start at 9 am, but that discussion is for a different book. We're all tempted to make sure our kids get up for school, and in fact I've heard of multiple parents who continue to call and wake up their kids even after the kid is in college. Just think about this for a second. Then let them set an alarm on the phone, which is embedded into their body anyway, or buy them this[15].

Budgeting

Let's face it, college is incredibly expensive. As parents, we bear the ever-rising price tag because we believe this experience will prove worth the price for our kids. That said, it's critical to teach kids the difference between necessities and luxuries, and to help them budget accordingly. Books, school supplies and a meal plan are all necessities. Going with your friends to clubs, concerts, etc. are not. Many students open credit cards in their own name at this point. This is a great way for them to learn, though you'll want to explain that what they charge, they'll eventually be paying for; yes, some teens otherwise will treat a charge card as found money.

Along the same lines, start giving your seniors more financial responsibility and autonomy. Kids need to learn how to manage their money (especially when coming to a wealthy school where there will always be students willing to go out more often

---

15 https://www.amazon.com/Umiin-Runaway-Alarm-Wheels-Sleepers/dp/B016F4A6Q2/ref=sr_1_1?ie=UTF8&qid=1475680673&sr=8-1-spons&keywords=alarm+clock+for+heavy+sleepers&psc=1

and spend money more freely, no pun intended). Having a head-start here will prove immensely useful once your student is confronting these decisions.

It's Their Major, Not Yours

A recent Washington Post story [16]written by Steven Pearlstein, a Professor of Public Affairs at George Mason University, was quite eye-opening. The article begins:

> "When I assigned an 800-page biography of Andrew Carnegie for a new undergraduate course on wealth and poverty at George Mason University a few years ago, I wasn't sure the students would actually read it. Not only did most of them make it to the end, however, but many thanked me for giving them the chance to read a popular work of history. Curious, I inquired how many were history majors. Of the 24 honors students in the seminar, there were none. English? Philosophy? Fine arts? Only one. How was this possible? I asked. Almost in unison, half a dozen replied: 'Our parents wouldn't let us.' The results were similar when I surveyed freshmen in another honors seminar this spring. This time, I asked how many would have been humanities majors if the only criteria were what they were interested in and what they were good at. Ten of the 24 raised their hands."

Yikes. I totally understand the idea of making sure our kids' college yields a return on the investment (ROI). College is super expensive, and my whole business is predicated on the notion that it's far too costly to waste it. Still, if the above sample is any indication of a wider trend, 9 of 10 students who would like to major in the humanities but don't are making this decision to please their parents.

There are whole treatises about helicopter parenting, so there's no need for me to lecture anyone here about the dangers of this style. Moreover, I'll discuss how the fallacy of the major leads to a job theory in Chapter 6. What's vital to keep in mind here is that ROI doesn't mean our kids need to get any job that pays them enough to justify the cost of the education we sprung for; ROI means they get jobs that leave them feeling energized and fulfilled, and where they can earn a living to support whatever lifestyle they require. If you disagree, and believe that only money matters, and that it's truly fine for your kids to end up miserable at work, as long as they make a lot of dough, then save yourselves the few hours it will take to finish this book and just toss it now.

---

16 https://www.washingtonpost.com/posteverything/wp/2016/09/02/meet-the-parents-who-wont-let-their-children-study-literature/?utm_term=.7bf2038cf503

You've Had Your Shot

Karl Gude, a Michigan State School of Journalism instructor and former Director of Information Graphics at Newsweek magazine, wrote a piece [17]which every parent should peruse. The money quote for me was this: "Most of my students love and respect their parents but are terrified to confront them or go against their wishes, which is the power dynamic the parents have set up in their family. They're also terrified of disappointing them. The students who come to me... basically a stranger... feel desperate, lost and hopeless. (Wouldn't it be nice if they could go to their own parents?) They feel they are being forced into a life they don't want and never will and worse, one that will strangle their uniqueness. Jim Morrison, lead singer of the "Doors," said it best, "'The most loving parents and relatives commit murder with smiles on their faces. They force us to destroy the person we really are... .'"

One other thought about this is to start early. It's incredibly difficult to suddenly shift the dynamic between parent and child in senior year of high school. Starting the process earlier allows for mistakes to get made, learning to occur, and for everyone to benefit accordingly.

Let Them Do Their Own Homework

This may strike some of you as obvious; others are saying, "Well, I just edit my daughter's papers," while some parents sheepishly admit to literally doing their kids' work. Here's the thing about that, though: you're not helping them, you're crippling them. In another *Washington Post* story, [18]Marla Vannucci, an associate professor at the Adler School of Professional Psychology in Chicago, described having "a college-aged client whose parents did her homework for her. The client's mother explained that she didn't want her daughter to struggle the same way she had. The daughter, however, 'has grown up to be an adult who has anxiety attacks anytime someone asks her to do something challenging' because she never learned how to handle anything on her own."

As a former employer of hundreds of recent college graduates, I can assure you that the ones who didn't last very often were unable to apply their training to their work, and had no mechanisms for dealing with the critiques that are inevitable when

17 http://www.huffingtonpost.com/karl-gude/parents-the-worst-kind-of_b_5097971.html
18 https://www.washingtonpost.com/news/parenting/wp/2014/09/02/how-helicopter-parents-are-ruining-college-students/?tid=sm_fb&utm_term=.b1ef25c61529

you start a job you know very little about. Conversely, successful employees exhibited a thick skin as well as the ability to overcome their initial lack of knowledge by learning to understand what was being asked of them, beyond just following a few specific tasks.

The aforementioned story discussed a study published by two professors from California State University Fresno. The authors of "Helicopter Parents: An Examination of the Correlates of Over-parenting of College Students," Jill C. Bradley-Geist and Julie B. Olson-Buchanan, asserted, "While parental involvement might be the extra boost that students need to build their own confidence and abilities, over-parenting appears to do the converse in creating a sense that one cannot accomplish things socially *or in general on one's own*," (emphasis added here) adding that "over-parenting can actually ruin a child's abilities to deal with the workplace."

According to another study,[19] this one published in the *Journal of Child and Family Studies* and led by Associate Professor of Psychology at the University of Mary Washington, Holly Schiffrin, "Parents are sending an unintentional message to their children that they are not competent." Schiffrin adds that competence and autonomy are consistence markers of future feelings of well-being, which clearly is every parent's goal for their child (i.e., to be happy).

Think of it this way: there's no employer that will want or allow an employee to have their parent do their work for them. At some point, kids need to work on their own, so the sooner they learn how, the better at it they'll be, and the more confidence they'll have in their abilities.

Resolving Conflicts is Hard but Doable

Most parents would agree that watching their kids struggle is painful. But "fixing" things for them is worse, according to a Florida State University study,[20] published in the *Journal of Child and Family Studies*. A *Real Simple* article discussing this indicated that the study "warns that overbearing parenting can not only keep children from developing into self-sufficient adults, but it can also make them depressed and anxious."

Of course this doesn't mean you won't be there to listen when your new college student is upset about a grade, or a roommate, or school in general. Listening, though, is very

---

19 http://link.springer.com/article/10.1007/s10826-013-9716-3

20 http://link.springer.com/article/10.1007/s10826-016-0466-x

different from interfering. Mallory Lucier-Greer, the author of the above-referenced study, said in *Real Simple*, "Parent's interactions with children play a large part in how a child views their own capabilities," adding, "If parents are simply being supportive, they are saying things like 'you can manage your finances, you can pick out your classes.' It changes if they are doing that all for you. I think there are good intentions behind those helicopter behaviors, but at the end of the day you need to foster your child's development."

Final Tips

1.   Less Talking, More Decision Making

     Rachel Simmons, Co-Founder of Girls Leadership Institute and the author of the New York Times bestsellers Odd Girl Out: The Hidden Culture of Aggression in Girls and The Curse of the Good Girl: Raising Authentic Girls with Courage and Confidence, wrote a thoughtful and thought-provoking piece[21] *for Time.com with the sub-heading,* "When a teen is having trouble, talking more about the issue isn't always the solution."

     Parents believe, and dare I say have been taught, that having a kid who speaks to us about his issues is a "parenting win." In this article, Simmons points to research indicating this might not be so.

     "Psychologists have identified a style of communication [termed co-rumination] between parents and adolescent children that can have the opposite effect of soothing. Co-rumination occurs when we dwell with our kids on their problems, worry about a problem's causes, focus on a child's negative feelings and egg each other on to keep talking. Originally discovered in 2002 as a phenomenon occurring among friends, co-ruminating … has been linked by University of Missouri psychologist Amanda Rose to both closeness in relationship and anxiety and depression."

     According to Simmons, repetitive talking about problems brings parents and kids closer, but it can also make kids unhappy. What's more, "Co-rumination

---

21 http://time.com/4031257/college-freshman-depression-parenting/

also interferes with people's ability and motivation to solve problems, too, largely because it's more about talking about challenges than taking action to address them. ..."

I'd return here to a brief goal analysis. If our goal as a parent is to have our children be super tight with us, then to hell with the co-rumination idea. But if we desire to ensure that our kids learn how to function as adults and how to maximize their potential and feeling of self-worth, then we need to back off.

Simmons addresses how to do this with a problem-solving method known as "ORID." I'll quote the example she cites in its entirety, as it is quite illuminating:

> Say your child is talking with you about a roommate she doesn't like. The roommate is inconsiderate and unfriendly and, on top of that, doesn't seem to realize she's a royal slob. Your daughter sounds despondent; it's only the second week of school. How will she survive for an entire academic year?
>
> Your first line of questions should be *objective*: Ask her what she actually knows to be true. What events have occurred? What has the roommate said and done? What did your daughter say or do in reply? Stick with the who, what, where, when and how. No whys. Don't let your daughter start editorializing (*Can you believe how rude she is? How am I going to study when he's so insanely loud?!*). Remain on the solid ground of evidence and what she knows to be true right now.
>
> Your next set of questions are *reflective*: How does she feel about this? Is she angry? Betrayed? Disappointed? Let her vent a bit about how the roommate assignment process is rigged, and whether pitching a tent on the quad is legal.
>
> Now, move to *interpretive* questions: What does this mean for her? What is the impact of having an inconsiderate, unfriendly roommate? How will that affect her emotionally, socially and academically?
>
> Finally, move to *decisional* questions: What is she going to do about this, and how can you help her? What campus resources are

available, and what's the best next step? Is it to confront her room-mate, talk to residence life staff, or try to switch rooms? What's the school's policy and protocol?

Simmons continues, "One sign that your child might prefer co-ruminating is that you get blown off when you direct him to the decisional questions. This is where you might hear, *It's hopeless. There's nothing I can do. I can't believe he left his dirty laundry on my bed!* Or: *I knew I should have gone to that other school.*

Here's what you might say in response: 'I know you're upset. I get it, and I would be, too. But at some point, we have to move forward, try to address what's happening and make this better for you. The best way for us to move forward is to figure out your next steps. Let's do that together.' Empathy will be key. When your child believes you really respect what he's feeling, he'll be much more likely to trust you."

Some other thoughts to consider:

Try not to internalize your child's feelings at that moment, because chances are your child may just be venting and will be over it the next day, especially if you handle the situation well.

Don't bring it up again unless your child does. Otherwise, you're encouraging them to ruminate, which is a part of co-ruminating. It may be more productive to ask about the actions/solutions taken to resolve the issue, if you feel this is necessary.

One final strategy is not picking up the phone immediately, each and every time your child calls. Listen to the voice mail to see what your child needs; you can always call right back if it's important. This strategy helps your child figure it out on his own. By the time you call back later, you may be surprised that it's no longer an issue. This also gives you a chance to figure out how to help with resolution and not co-ruminate.

2. Let Them Have Some Secrets

The questions described in this story [22] mostly have one thing in common: they're incredibly judgmental. As indicated repeatedly above, all parents want what's best for their kids, and most parents believe that they know what that it is, based on their experience. Taking this one step further, it's true that many times parents are 100% right. We know that going out too much, not sleeping and eating a whole pizza at 3 am after having shots and beers isn't the healthiest lifestyle. Still, for our kids to develop, they have to

---

22 https://www.society19.com/10-questions-parents-stop-asking-college-students/

learn some of these things on their own, unfortunately. As it turns out, they often know what's best for themselves, and we're wrong. So cut them some slack, and be there to listen if they do decide to bring up a problem.

3. Read

Books I'd suggest all parents read:

> *Excellent Sheep: The Miseducation of the American Elite and the Way to a Meaningful Life,*[23] by William Deresiewicz

> *How to Raise an Adult,*[24] by former Stanford dean Julie Lythcott-Haims

> *The Price of Privilege,*[25] by Madeline Levine, psychologist, who describes three ways we might be "over-parenting and unwittingly causing psychological harm:"

> 1. When we do for our kids what they can *already* do for themselves.
> 2. When we do for our kids what they can *almost* do for themselves.
> 3. When our parenting behavior is motivated by our own egos.

According to Levine, when we parent this way "we deprive our kids of the opportunity to be creative, to problem solve, to develop coping skills, to build resilience, to figure out what makes them happy, to figure out who they are. ... Although we over-involve ourselves to protect our kids and it may in fact lead to short-term gains, our behavior actually delivers the rather soul-crushing news: *Kid, you can't actually do any of this without me.*"

The information and resources presented here are by no means exhaustive. Still, I'm confident that parents using these techniques will greatly ease the transition between their kids' existing home, and their new home. Enjoy.

---

23 https://www.amazon.com/dp/1476702721/?tag=slatmaga-20

24 https://www.amazon.com/How-Raise-Adult-Overparenting-Prepare/dp/1250093635/ref=sr_1_1?ie=UTF8&qid=1475680308&sr=8-1&keywords=How+to+Raise+an+Adult

25 https://www.amazon.com/dp/006059585X/?tag=slatmaga-20

CHAPTER 3

Bucket Lists: Your GPS

Y ou get in your car, turn it on, adjust the mirrors, and the GPS appears. It knows where you are now; it simply asks for your destination. How far do you get if you enter "no idea"? Do you even make it out of the driveway?

Setting no course whatsoever is the typical plan executed by the vast majority of college students. Unfortunately, it's not a plan at all, and worse, leads to many students fumbling around, hoping they accidentally discover what they like and are good at doing. Worse still is that a huge percentage of young adults are still in this mode, i.e. deeply unsatisfied with their jobs but having no idea how to address it. (Half the respondents in authors Richard Arum's and Josipa Roksa's recent study[26] reported that they lacked clear goals or a sense of direction TWO YEARS after graduation.) The problem at this point is they've already used up their college eligibility, in a way, and now have bills to pay and in the case of those earning a good living, a lifestyle (dinners out, vacations, nice clothes) to which they've grown accustomed. Two years becomes five years mighty quickly, and five years can turn into a lifetime in a heartbeat.

In a famous quote from Mary Tyler Moore, a TV show no one under 45 has ever heard of, Ted Baxter, played by the incomparable Ted Knight (the judge in Caddyshack) asks his boss, Lou (Ed Asner – you may know him as the voice of the main character in Up) why no one likes him. Lou responds, "Ted, do you know the way you are? Well, don't be that way."

Don't be the kid with no plan at all. College is an incredible place that you'll never get back; maximize your time there. To do so, you'll need to create some goals. Since most kids pucker up like someone just smashed a grapefruit in their eye when they hear the word goals, we'll use the term bucket lists (special shout out to my first mentee, Ian Bullard, from RU).

---

26 http://press.uchicago.edu/ucp/books/book/chicago/A/bo19088566.html

A side note before you begin: I've set out examples below that were presented by freshmen and sophomores in college. Obviously, your lists will change as you go through college. Juniors' and seniors' lists contain far more references to jobs and internships, as well as specific companies or industries with which they hope to get involved, than those presented by students in their first year or two of college.

Your bucket list should be broken down into three categories:

1. Basic Goals (things I need to do this semester).
2. Challenge Goals (things I'd like to do this semester but I'm not sure if I can).
3. Dream Goals (things I'd love to do this semester, regardless of how unrealistic they may seem).

Bucket lists are extremely personal, and so giving specific examples of the various goals can be a bit tricky. Let's dive in with some anyway.

1. Basic Goals (things I need to do this semester)

1. Get a 3.2 GPA, because the scholarship I'm on mandates this as a minimum.
2. Make 2-3 friends.
3. Get out of my room often, no matter the purpose.
4. Balance social life with school work.
5. Stay healthy and rested, with good habits and schedules.

2. Challenge Goals (things I'd like to do this semester but I'm not sure if I can)

1. Make Dean's list.
2. Figure out a major that appeals to me.
3. Find a side job of some sort to pay for gas (or Uber) and going out.
4. Join at least one club, and if possible, lead one and recruit members ... really foster a community.
5. Focus only on what I truly care about and determine which classes/clubs are not for me.
6. Play intramurals even in a sport I'm not that good at.
7. Interact with at least one professor.

8. Become a better writer; write a blog or for the school paper, or freelance for a site I like.
9. Get a summer internship.

3. Dream Goals (things I'd love to do this semester, regardless of how unrealistic they may seem)

1. Get a 4.0 GPA.
2. Create an awesome company, work with one, or design a killer app or product.
3. Learn to code.
4. Become president of my dorm.
5. Master public speaking so much that I seek it out.

You'll observe with these lists that some things are must dos, while others can slide between the categories depending on your personality. Getting a certain GPA to maintain a paid scholarship is a must; getting a 4.0 isn't. And for some people, getting a 4.0 might not even be a dream, as for many students, this simply isn't that important when compared to learning other skills. Everyone benefits from having the lists, though:

1. Dramatically improve your sense of self-achievement. When you do things for yourself, not for your parents, or for your teachers, or for your friends, you'll feel amazing once you've ticked these items off your list.

2. By forcing yourself to set both challenge and dream goals, you'll be forced to think more ambitiously. Imagine if you achieve any of these goals; imagine if you surpass some. With work and some good fortune, you will. And even if you don't, you'll have succeeded. For if you are working hard, taking classes that interest you, and actively participating in class discussions, you'll be building the habits you'll need in the dreaded real world, even if you don't get all A's or achieve every dream you wrote down.

3. Learn about yourself and eliminate things you no longer care about. Let's say you joined your school's student government, because you did this in H.S. and always liked it. One semester into it you realize the student government has no power whatsoever, and that no one takes it seriously. You decide not to do it anymore.

Was this a waste? Far from it. It's similar to when you take that accounting class, for instance, in that one part of you thinks this might be a good career, but after one class, you learn that you'd rather walk around campus in a Marriott bathrobe than do more accounting. You haven't lost; you've saved yourself from years of work in a field you hate. That's huge, and in a sense, is irreplaceable.

If you don't believe me, maybe you'll trust Richard J. Light, a professor at Harvard Graduate School of Education and author of "Making the Most of College." In a *New York Times* article[27] from mid-2015, Professor Light describes an exercise he has students undertake. ".... We ask students to make a list of how they want to spend their time at college. What matters to you? This might be going to class, studying, spending time with close friends, perhaps volunteering in the off-campus community or reading books not on any course's required reading list. Then students make a list of how they actually spent their time, on average, each day over the past week and match the two lists. Finally, we pose the question: How well do your commitments actually match your goals? A few students find a strong overlap between the lists. The majority don't. They are stunned and dismayed to discover they are spending much of their precious time on activities they don't value highly. The challenge is how to align your time commitments to reflect your personal convictions."

I couldn't have said it better myself, folks. And so I didn't even try.

Homework

1. Create a blueprint: write down your goals and dreams, as well as a plan to achieve them. Print this out, and keep it in your pocket.

2. Once a week, compare what you're spending your time on to your blueprint. Adjust your actions accordingly.

3. Share a goal or two with a friend. Sometimes having another person encourage or prod you can provide the motivation you need if your energy fades.

4. When you hit a challenge or dream goal, treat yourself and a friend to a big old ice cream sundae, or something else you don't normally have.

---

27 https://www.nytimes.com/2015/08/02/education/edlife/how-to-live-wisely.html?smid=pl-share&_r=0

CHAPTER 4

Common Fears and Solutions: YOU ARE NOT ALONE

T alk to incoming college freshmen and you'll learn that many share the same worries:

How will I make friends when I'm terrible at small talk?

How am I supposed to manage my time? How much studying will I need to do?

I'm not as smart as the other kids and I don't belong here. What if I fail?

As stated in the title of this chapter: you're not alone. Government statistics indicate that in 2015, approximately 13 MILLION kids were attending 4 year colleges. What does that mean to you as a freshman? That means that more than 3 million other people are going through largely the same things as you are, right now.

So why do you feel so alone with these worries? Because your peers won't fess up to feeling the same way. A good part of the reason people feel badly about being nervous is thinking that feeling that way is itself weird and wrong. Feeling somewhat nervous about this enormous transition, amongst the biggest if not THE biggest transition you'll ever make, is not weird; not feeling any nerves, I'd argue, would be pretty strange. So step one in overcoming your nerves is to accept that it's OK to feel them.

Step two in the adjustment process is deciding not to give into your nerves. Accept that you have them, sure. But lay in bed feeling out of sorts? Not OK.

Like with everything else I'll discuss in this book, the keys to doing better and feeling better lie in specific tactics, not in clichés or aphorisms (you are in college, so if you don't know the word aphorism, look it up). So here we go:

How To Make Friends

A huge fear of a surprisingly large number of incoming college freshmen is how they will find new friends. This makes a great deal of sense, actually, considering that the last time most college freshmen made new friends was in middle school, seven years earlier; it's no surprise that you'd be out of practice. Adding homesickness to the mix obviously doesn't help. But since almost everyone is in the same position (some just hide their fears better), one would presume that the problem simply works itself out. For many kids, it does. But for a substantial amount of students, friend-making, often a critical step to feeling truly engaged on campus, remains difficult; for others, it takes far longer than it has to. And as this problem is beyond the "skills" of even the most adept helicopter parent pilots, students really are on their own to address it.

Having spoken to countless upperclassmen, almost all of whom went through this very issue, I've learned that there are a few methods freshmen can use to accelerate the process of fitting in and finding friends:

Orientation

Colleges are invested in students sticking around, prompting the freshman orientation (and sometimes even pre-orientation) period. Take advantage of these opportunities, as everyone with whom you'll interact is in exactly your shoes. My close friend from college met his future wife at orientation; you don't need to do that to be successful, but even a modicum of friendliness will yield you huge rewards.

Just Say Hi

"What do I even say to other kids?" is a common question asked by nervous incoming freshmen. Suggestion: Just say "Hi." At orientation. In class. On those long, winding college paths. In the dining hall. At the gym. And especially in your dorm, both on your floor and elsewhere, as these are the kids you'll initially see most often. Remember that most of the people you'll be meeting feel as awkward about this as you do. So start with the basics, and be open to these conversations.

That said, most small talk sucks. So don't make small talk. Actually ask a question where you're interested in hearing the answer. Then follow up with something about yourself that's on topic; it can be something minor, too, as getting too intense too soon isn't the best move either. Still, this is real talk, and surprisingly, it works. Also worth noting is that the first friend group you make almost certainly won't be your last. So there's no need to worry about latching on too tightly, and you don't need to be perfect with every person you meet. College is not high school. If your first crowd gets you through month one, that's great. As you find other people, you can disengage with group one if they're not really your type.

How Do I Find the Party?

Yes, parents, kids in college party. But knowing where to go gets stressful. Some tips my college friends have shared include asking the athletes, who often know what's happening; speaking with older kids; or simply asking the kids in your dorm where they are going. I promise that pretty soon "Where are you headed tonight, mind if I tag along?" turns into "Where are we going tonight?"

Join Clubs

While no one can guarantee that you'll make tons of friends by joining clubs, I can guarantee that you won't meet any sitting in your room playing video games or surfing social media by yourself. In fact, the more actively engaged you are in any of the tons of clubs every college offers, the more your friend base (and future network) expands. The best part about this is that you'll meet kids who are not exactly like you but who do share at least one of your interests; the more friend groups you make, the less lonely you'll feel.

So go out for intramurals or club teams in any of the sports you like to play, even if you weren't your H.S. team's captain. Join the debate team or student government. Become a tour guide. Form an entrepreneur's society, an art club, or whatever you like. Do five of these things, and then drop the ones that aren't cutting it. Wash, rinse, repeat.

Try Something New

It's certainly easier for all of us to do the things we've always done; that's why the term comfort zone exists. Limiting ourselves to these comfort zones cuts us off from meeting people who may end up as our best friends. My roommate in college was (and is) a fantastic guitar player. I am tone deaf. I had gone to one concert in my life prior to college, and didn't see music as my path to anything. But listening to my roommate play, I came to appreciate his skill and persistence. This led to watching his band perform, and even to taking road trips with them. My roommate and I would have been friends regardless; his band members and I never would have met had I not immersed myself a bit in their music.

Quoting my insightful friend Eric Kriftcher on this topic, "Get[ting] out of your comfort zone is a way to ... tap into an additional network of friends. If you're not inclined to the arts, go to a concert or show or see if you can encourage someone to go with you. The same if you're not an athlete [go to a game]. Go to a lecture on a topic that you don't know much about. Take advantage of all the school offers, not just the limited universe with which you're familiar."

How Do I Manage My Time? How Much Studying Is Enough?

For the first time, you'll be "free" to choose what you do every day. For a lot of people, this is liberating, but also terrifying. Sure, having your parents nag you about your hygiene, your homework and when you were going to be home was annoying. But that nagging established a structure you got used to, and that you now don't have (if your parents are still nagging you about your hygiene and your homework, we have bigger problems to discuss). You're on your own, free to oversleep and miss class, free to not turn in assignments, free to stay up until 5AM. Doing any or all of these things at times may not lead to any lasting problems. Doing them all the time definitely will.

So my watchword here is balance. Balance your school work and study time with your social activities. Balance both of these things with the clubs you join, the jobs you take, and the sleep you need to keep all this going. Keep adjusting - every week, every month, every semester - according to what's important to you at the time, and based on what's working. Remember to look at your bucket lists, as this will be your roadmap of sorts. If you set a goal of becoming vice president of the marketing club, and you realize this will take five hours a week versus the two hours you'd been devoting to this club before, then you'll need to find three hours somewhere. This might come out of the time you spend doing nothing much of anything, but sometimes it can't; in the latter instance, something else will need to give. Or you can adjust your bucket list, if you determine you have too many things on it. The good news, even if it doesn't always seem that way, is that the choice is yours.

As for studying, one thing all schools have in common is their desire to keep the students they accept from failing out. Given that, schools will go to great lengths to provide academic counseling and tutoring to anyone who needs it. Take advantage of this; you (and/or your parents) are paying for it anyway.

I rarely talk about my own college experiences, as I don't think they're all that relevant given the decades (ugh) since they occurred.

I'm making an exception here regarding studying. By reviewing only the material I already knew, I managed to get a 44 on my first Calculus test. Hearing this, my brother, who was a year ahead of me, "offered" to tutor me (translation: He said, "You're coming over twice a week until you know this stuff better than the teacher.") Every week, I reluctantly trudged over to his campus, where he indeed taught me the material impeccably. After I got a 99 on the second test, the teacher actually accused me of cheating. I was only able to extricate myself by suggesting that he ask me any question he wanted, as I was confident I'd know the answer. So if you don't want to avail yourselves of the school services, you better hope you have a genius brother willing to waste his time on you.

I'll share one more experience that I believe stands the test of time. I vividly recall every day passing these two guys in the hallway, which was sort of a lounge, in our dorm, splayed out with books all over the table, assorted caffeinated drinks and salty snacks at the ready. I'd see them at 9AM; they'd still be there at 9PM when I was going out. Midway through the semester, one of them asked, "How come we never see you studying?" My reply was, "If you saw me studying, I wouldn't be studying."

Study in private. Isolation leads to concentration. Find the most boring place on campus, where no one goes, and study there. Hint: this may not be the library. Fear of missing out (FOMO) is a real thing, and you'll definitely miss out on socializing while you study. But trust me, you'll have far more time to hang out if you study in private. What's more, you'll get better grades in the process.

I'm Not Smart/What If I Fail?

Most college students have done fairly well in H.S. Many have excelled. Going to college is the first time a lot of you will truly meet your equals, and even people who are smarter. (My friend Tara always says she's still waiting for this last part to happen, but she's smart enough to recognize one day it might.) But because some kids are smarter doesn't make you suddenly stupid. Moreover, other people's intellect will have little to no bearing on your success. You control your grades, and as discussed above, you have the techniques needed to do well. More importantly, you control which classes you select. If you've determined through trial and error that Chemistry isn't for you, don't take it. You're not in college to impress anyone else, nor will the vast majority of your future employers ever care about what classes you had. They will care that you applied yourself, that you learned how to learn, and that you maximized whatever innate skills you have. Those are translatable skills. Being better than your peers at memorizing the Periodic Table isn't.

The second aspect of this insecurity surrounds the idea of "failing." Again, most of you have probably never failed, at anything, but especially not in your classes; this can make getting a C for the first time seem like a tragedy. While I wouldn't advocate getting Cs as a goal, you shouldn't consider yourself dumb and unworthy if you get some. The key will be knowing why it happened. If you got a C in a class where had you actually tried you'd have gotten an A, well then we all know that's not a good thing. But let's say you took a shot at Coding, just to see if you might like it. It turns out it's hard as hell, and you stink at it. Somehow, even giving it your all yields only a C+. Should this be deemed a failure? Not only is my answer no, but also I'd argue this is a huge success. Why? Because determining early on what you might be really interested in, and what you're good at, saves you years of heartache later. Think of the nursing student who in junior year finally goes for hospital training, only to discover he/she faints at the sight of blood. (Even this is better than the kid who pursues a career in, say, investment banking, then realizes five years after college that he actually hates finance). Self-discovery early is huge, so never let fear of "failing" stand in your way of achieving it.

Finally, I can't discuss this topic without mentioning the obvious: the idea that other people think you are stupid implies they are actually paying attention to you, the way they did (or seemingly did) in middle school and high school. College isn't like that. Your fellow students don't remember you as the kid who puked on the desk in 8th grade, or who cried when the teacher called on you in class. They don't recall all those little embarrassing moments you've tried so hard to forget. They don't remember or recall anything about you, BECAUSE THEY DON'T KNOW YOU AT ALL. The most amazing thing about college is everyone gets a clean slate. You can be who you were, who you are, who you want to be, or whomever, and no one else will know the difference. And incredibly, they also won't give a shit. Why? Everyone else is worrying about themselves. This is the biggest advantage to being amongst a group of 18-21 year-olds; your inherent self-absorption actually works in your favor when it comes to being judged. So don't be embarrassed if you say an answer in class and it's wrong. This won't cause the Internet to blow up. Failing is essential, not bad. If you never fail, it means you really aren't trying to succeed.

So go ahead and try out for a dance troupe or music group, speak up in a lecture, and take a class that seems interesting but hard. No one cares if you mess up, and you just might find that you're great at something that you never considered before.

Homework

1. Ask people in your dorm to lunch until someone says yes. Do that every day.

2. Find the most boring place on campus. Study there.

3. When you identify a friend you can trust, share when you're nervous about a class. If that goes well, and your friend proves to be a good listener, make sure you return the favor.

4. Go to a game, a concert, a lecture, or anything that's different from what you've done before.

CHAPTER 5

Picking Classes

I t's May in your senior year of H.S., you've chosen a college, and you're thinking to yourself, "Wow, I'm glad that's over." Kudos.

But before you know it, you'll be confronting the first major decision of your college life, one that like many others you'll be making with, at best, incomplete information: selecting classes. Sure, if you're pre-med or a budding engineer, your choices will be limited. For the liberal arts student, however, perusing the school course catalog is like looking at a 14-page diner menu, except you can't escape the angst that too many choices yields (lobster, lamb chops, spaghetti, hot dogs, and open-faced turkey – really?) by just ordering "the usual."

What can you do to narrow down the seemingly endless options available to you?

- **Take What Excites You.** If you have any interest in a topic, take a class to discover whether you really like it. Really enjoyed AP History? Take an introduction to world history class. Worked for the school paper? By all means, explore a writing course. Think you want to be in finance, or accounting? Take them. At worst, you'll cross off topics that no longer get you jazzed. At best, you'll discover that what you previously liked, you now actually love, leading to a possible major course of study. And as my always introspective sister points out, "Your unique talents and interests could lead you to a major and career you've never heard of ... another reason to read the coursework for the various majors!"

- **Check your school's add/drop policy.** Most schools offer a "shopping period" in which, without negative consequences, you can try a number of classes for a short time before eliminating those that don't capture your attention. Just be sure you know exactly how long this period lasts; academic advisors and even upperclassmen can be essential here.

- **Tests. Papers. Reading. Writing. Memorization.** Something few people initially consider when picking classes is balancing the requirements you'll face in total. You may love psychology, and philosophy, and history; if you take classes in all three of these subjects in one semester, you may find yourself burdened with many hundreds of pages of reading a week. For some people this might be fine, but if you know you're not one of them, then space out your classes accordingly. Mix in a mandatory language class, where memorization is all that'll matter. Throw in an accounting class, which might have difficult tests but which won't have a ton of reading. Find a writing class, where you won't have tests or heavy reading to do. Strike a balance.

- **Teamwork. Writing. Speaking.** Anything you do as an adult will require elements of these three things. There's no better time to learn and improve your abilities in these areas than in college. (If you believe hiring managers, and you kinda have to, college graduates may not be as prepared to work as they think.) Take classes that force you to do group projects, those where you'll need to write papers, and especially those that have you doing presentations. Even if you're not adept at these skills when you start, you'll certainly need them later, and you cannot get better at these skills without practice. Awkward? Yes. Uncomfortable? Yes. Invaluable? Also, yes.

Let's explore these three areas more fully.

Teamwork

At first blush, you may think, "I've played on teams or participated in groups my whole life so I definitely get it." And on one level, sports and other activities certainly help.

However, I think what hiring managers try to identify are people who do fine relating to those who are exactly like them, but not so fine dealing with those who are different.

An easy way of learning how to reconcile differences is to take classes that require group projects. Admittedly, these projects can be dreadful. From motivating the inevitable slackers to dialing back the bullies, from establishing the alphas to marshaling everyone's schedules, group dynamics are always different and challenging. But that's the whole point. Fighting through these difficulties is how you'll ascertain how groups work, under pressure, when it matters. This is an absolute must skill to develop, as when you enter the workforce, your ability to actively engage as a team member will be a huge part of what your co-workers use to evaluate you.

(Another way of addressing this, outside the classroom, is to get a job, any job, but particularly one where you are with older people, people of different colors, people of different genders and people of different socioeconomic backgrounds. Deal with these people. Learn how to work with them. This is what your life after school will be; trust me, your workplace won't look like your sorority or even your dorm. Might as well learn it now.)

Writing

The task of every written message you send is to get people's attention, to get them to do something for you – in a way that isn't arrogant and yet is effective. Once you enter the workforce, the importance of written communications, whether they be emails to your colleagues and bosses (yes folks, emails are still the preferred mode of communication in most jobs, at least for now), written presentations to prospective customers, or even texts to an underling, multiplies. You will be hard pressed to find a job where you can be seen as valuable if your writing sucks.

How to do it: Take classes that make you write papers, not just expository writing or mandatory freshman English 101. Examine the syllabi and ask other students to determine which classes feature some paper writing. Then take a few of them.

The second part of this process is to meet with your professors to discuss your papers. When a professor comments on something you've written, the fastest way for you to get better is to review the comments with the professor, in person. Even if a professor doesn't comment, discussing your writing with them will absolutely make you a better writer. (In Chapter 9, we'll discuss methods to make these interactions less awkward.)

As a person who edited reports for decades, a few writing skills are paramount:

1. Know basic skills like using spell check and understanding the difference between "your" and "you're." These kinds of mistakes, even if they appear innocent, can paint you as lazy and even dumb. Harsh? I suppose, but when a

business sends a client a proposal that contains errors like these, the prospect doesn't say, "Oh, I bet Ashley is a really great person who just can't write. Let's buy $1m worth of stuff from her company right away."

2. Use punctuation. Please, please, please learn the difference between a comma and a semi-colon. I recognize I sound like my high school expository writing teacher, Mr. Williamson, but he was right; run-on sentences just sound bad, and are confusing. If you're not sure of the difference, look it up, or ask a tutor. This will be well worth the minimal effort you'll expend.

3. Make a point. As Steve Martin said to John Candy in Planes, Trains and Automobiles, "When you're telling a story, have a point. It makes it a lot more interesting for the listener." (I imagine most of you haven't even heard of this movie, much less seen it. If so, put this book down now and find it on Hulu, Netflix, Amazon Prime or wherever. I promise you it holds up.) Making a point is imperative in writing as well. Don't bury the lead. Think about the goal of your message, and organize your thoughts to accomplish this goal. This cannot be over-stressed. When you don't have a goal, your writing will meander. That may be fine in poetry, but in business writing, people aren't looking for sonnets or haikus.

4. Predict the future. Every time you compose a message, put yourself in the reader's shoes and think about how they are likely to react. (This is a message from a professor who I respect and admire.) I'm not denigrating how difficult this can be. The value of developing this skill, though, is enormous. If I'm telling a client that my product is going to cost more than I originally indicated it would, I absolutely need to first accept that this message is not going to be received happily. Given that, I must frame the communication in a way that minimizes the expected displeasure. Suppose I'm the caterer handling a huge corporate holiday party. How might my customer react if they received this email: "John, the price for the event where we quoted you $5,000 is now going to be $8,500. Sorry." Alternatively, what if I sent this: "John, as you may have noticed, the market price of lobster has skyrocketed since you booked this event six months ago. If we keep lobster on your menu I'm afraid you'd be unhappy with the cost. We have some amazing shrimp and crab recipes, which I think your team will love and which we can provide at the original price. Let us know how you'd like us to proceed, and we'll do so at once."

Which of these do you think will make my customer feel like I understand what's happening, and that I'm actually looking out for his best interests? That's a skill worth learning.

The hidden upside of learning to write effectively is that not only will this make you more confident, it also will make you more employable. Furthermore, back to course selection, remember it's also actually easier for most people to have a mix of class requirements (i.e. test, papers, presentations) than to have all tests.

Speaking

Public speaking is like drinking water, if the water was from a polluted creek. It's absolutely necessary to learn how to keep people interested in what you're saying, but it can be painful to get through.

I've seen quite a few people recommend that students take acting or even improvisation classes. I love the premise, but I fear that practically, few people will do either.

So what's an easier way? Take classes that force you to do presentations. I get it; it's super awkward. At first. But once you practice, you'll improve, and even if you never become Abe Lincoln, making oratorical history, you'll get competent enough (and confident enough) to perform well during job interviews that come your way in the future.

It may not be possible to determine what classes will have you doing presentations merely by reading course descriptions. This is where academic advisors, older students and even sites like ratemyprofessor.com can come in handy. Additionally, many marketing and communications courses will have you speaking in front of your class, and are therefore worth considering even if those topics don't necessarily appeal to you.

Even just speaking up in any class is useful.

Adam Grant, magician turned workplace author (check out https://www.amazon.com/Originals-How-Non-Conformists-Move-World/dp/0525429565), [28]asserted in an interview[29] with the New York Times, "We all have original ideas. ...Most of us [just] don't act on these ideas. We're afraid we're going to be rejected or ridiculed ..."

---

28 https://www.amazon.com/Originals-How-Non-Conformists-Move-World/dp/0525429565
29 https://www.nytimes.com/2016/02/07/business/adam-grant-a-workplace-magician-reveals-his-secrets.html?_r=1

Probably the most overlooked benefit of being in college is that you can speak your mind, with little fear of consequences. You're not yet supporting a family, or worried you're about to lose your job if you look stupid.

So if you have anything to add to a discussion, whether in class, at an internship, on a job or at a club, by all means, speak up. What's the worst that can happen?

Finally, no discussion of public speaking and verbal and non-verbal communication is complete without mentioning my dear friend and renowned public speaking expert, Professor Chuck Garcia of Mercy College. Every student (and really, every employee) needs to read Chuck's book[30] on communication tactics. I promise you that it's replete with gems that will completely shift what you think you know about public speaking, and easily make any of you who reads it a much better presenter. Plus, it's brief, so there's no moaning allowed about it being too long.

As a teaser, here are three tips I plucked from a piece Chuck authored entitled, **"10 WAYS TO CHANGE YOUR ATTITUDE TOWARD PUBLIC SPEAKING:"**[31]

1. **SET REALISTIC GOALS**: Stop demanding that everything be perfect. Strive for progress, not perfection. One step at a time up that mountain!

2. **SELF-CONFIDENCE**: Keep telling yourself you are either a terrible or great speaker. Either way you're guaranteed to be right!

3. **TAKE IT FOR A TEST RUN**: When preparing, try your speech in front of 3 people you trust to provide constructive criticism. The adjustments made improve your presentation and boost your confidence.

I'll end by saying that there's no prouder moment for a student than overcoming a fear of public speaking. And in case anyone misses the other, obvious point, until job interviews are conducted using telepathy, it's always a good thing to learn how to present yourself verbally, even if it's only to one person.

---

30 https://www.amazon.com/Climb-Top-Communication-Leadership-Tactics/dp/1599326884

31 https://www.linkedin.com/pulse/attitude-determines-your-altitude-10-tips-change-toward-chuck-garcia?trk=eml-b2_content_ecosystem_digest-network_publishes-337-null&midToken=AQHboCURi3D xlg&fromEmail=fromEmail&ut=2QnaBudLYSx6U1

Homework

1. Try a class in Shakespeare, evolutionary biology, or creative writing before you decide on a major. Read through the course descriptions and pick something that sounds bizarre.

2. Run towards, rather than away from, that freshman English class that demands you write a lot of papers.

3. Discuss your papers with your teachers, especially when they've commented on what you've written.

4. Ask an upperclassman in your dorm which classes feature group projects and oral presentations. Take those classes that even remotely intrigue you.

CHAPTER 6

Picking a Major. Let the Fun Begin.

Before delving into the nitty gritty of selecting a major, an overview is warranted:

1. Most schools will want/demand you select a major by the end of sophomore year. This might sound intimidating at first, but what it really means is that you don't need to pick one before you even step on campus. Freshmen: Stop worrying.

2. You may pick a major and then later, switch to another one. You may even do this twice. Switching majors does not mean you've wasted time, as some students and parents fear. In contrast, this can be the best thing that's ever happened to you; imagine instead of switching from something you hate, you stuck with it, then got a job doing that same dreaded thing. Then imagine doing this for a decade. Or more. Suddenly the idea of switching while you still can to avert this awful outcome sounds more attractive, huh?

3. For most liberal arts majors, your major won't really matter to your future employers. I realize this is a radical statement, and that some folks (particularly my peers, most of whom graduated 30+ years ago into a totally different job market and haven't interviewed, much less hired, a young person since) disagree, but I've asked a lot of companies, and the consensus is that your ability to learn, to write, to speak, to work with various peers, to handle time pressures, and to be thick-skinned, are all critical. Whether your degree says B.A. in Philosophy or it says B.A. in History, eh, not so much. Most liberal arts

majors, at best, check a box for an interviewer. These kinds of majors are not differentiators. Skills and demeanor are.

While the major you choose often won't matter, your coursework might, depending on your field of interest. If you determine that want to work on Wall Street, take some economics courses even if you're a philosophy major. If you're an English major thinking of graduate school for psychology, obviously certain psychology classes will be necessary.

4. The idea that a Liberal Arts/Humanities major means you're relegated to eating canned soup for dinner for the rest of your life is absolutely absurd. According to Professor Pearlstein, "It's worth remembering that at American universities, the original rationale for majors was not to train students for careers. Rather, the idea was that after a period of broad intellectual exploration, a major was supposed to give students the experience of mastering one subject, in the process developing skills such as discipline, persistence, and how to research, analyze, communicate clearly and think logically.

As it happens, those are precisely the skills business executives still say they want from college graduates — although, to be fair, that has not always been communicated to their human-resource departments or the computers they use to sort through résumés. A study[32] for the Association of American Colleges and Universities found that 93 percent of employers agreed that a 'demonstrated capacity to think critically, communicate clearly, and solve complex problems is more important than [a job candidate's] undergraduate major.'"

Perhaps you're thinking, "What does this guy know?" That's a valid question, as maybe I'm basing too much on what my own company and numerous other people I know who hire young people for a living say. Maybe. Maybe it's easier to take the word of an Ivy League dean? In an article entitled, "If Students Are Smart, They'll Major in What They Love," [33] Cecilia Gaposchkin, an Associate Professor of History and Assistant Dean of faculty for pre-major advising at Dartmouth College, averred, "It's that time of

---

32 http://www.aacu.org/sites/default/files/files/LEAP/2013_EmployerSurvey.pdf

33 http://www.chronicle.com/article/If-Students-Are-Smart/230307/

year again: At many colleges, second-year students must declare their majors. Uncles, grandmothers, and friends will almost certainly ask: "What are you going to do with *that*?" Some parents will say, 'I am not going to shell out this amount of money for my kid to major in ....'"

"Such responses are based on the premise that choosing a major amounts to choosing a career path, and thus a particular financial future, a degree of security, a lifestyle, an entire identity. .... As it is often understood, the decision is loaded in ways that are not useful for the student or for the mission of higher education."

"As professors and academic advisers, we must be mindful of how pervasive these misconceptions are. We should take every opportunity to offer guidance to our students as they make these decisions. The premise that choosing a major is choosing a career rests on the faulty notion that 'the major' is important for its content, and that the acquisition of that content is what's valuable — meaning valuable to employers."

"But information is fairly easy to acquire. And much of the information acquired in 2015 will be obsolete by 2020. What is valuable is not the content of a major, but rather the ability to think with and through that information. That is the aim of a liberal-arts education, no matter the major."

"Ask employers. Company representatives who recruit at my college consistently say they don't really care about someone's major. What they want are basic but difficult-to-acquire skills. When they ask students about their majors, it's usually not because they want to assess the applicants' mastery of the content, but rather because they want to know if the students can talk about what they learned. They care about a potential employee's abilities: writing, researching, quantitative, and analytical skills. Some majors teach and hone some of these skills more than others do. Some career paths will use some more than others. But almost all white-collar jobs will require writing, communication, assessment, numeracy, and above all the creative application of knowledge."

"By releasing students from the pressure of the practical major and allowing them to study what they are sincerely interested in, we allow them to become smarter, more creative, and more able. This is what potential employers value, not course content that is likely to be obsolete once they have finished training the recent graduate."

Then there's this: a study[34] for the Association of American Colleges and Universities found that 93 percent of employers agreed that a "demonstrated capacity to think critically, communicate clearly, and solve complex problems is more important than [a job candidate's] undergraduate major."

With the above in mind, let's move on to how you can go about picking a major that's a fit for you:

1. Self-Knowledge.

    Start with the classes you liked in high school. The key is to separate out the material you found interesting from teachers you liked (or didn't). It's more sensible to take classes where you loved the material, despite the teacher, instead of the reverse.

2. Listen to Yourself, Not to Everyone Else.

    Take classes that you find appealing, even if your peers and parents question your choices. Of course you'll need to fit these classes in with whatever courses your school requires you to take, but even so there's often a fair amount of leeway for you to find classes that interest you. Pursuing your interests will lead to skills and passions.

3. Don't Think About Your Future Job Yet.

    The above point bears repeating: pursuing your interests will lead to skills and passions. And your confidence will soar with each new skill you develop. This is where your focus should be. Andy Chan, the Vice President for Personal and Career Development at Wake Forest University, is considered a "pioneer in a new wave of thinking about college career counseling." As mentioned in this story,[35] "his approach focuses less on steering students to jobs and more for preparing them for what employers will need. 'I teach students not to think about industries first,' Chan says. 'I teach them to think about skills and functions.'"

---

34 http://www.aacu.org/sites/default/files/files/LEAP/2013_EmployerSurvey.pdf

35 https://www.washingtonpost.com/lifestyle/magazine/starting-college-heres-how-to-graduate-with-a-job/2013/08/09/06805f36-ea79-11e2-a301-ea5a8116d211_story.html?utm_term=.93c621c6a94b

4. Read.

Carefully peruse course descriptions. Actually spend the time going through what the school has provided, instead of skimming. This is no place to skim.

5. Self-Knowledge Time, Again.

Once you've taken a variety of classes, examine what you enjoyed, and why. When you're selecting classes for your next semester, you'll discard some you previously thought sounded engaging while adding others based on the data you've accumulated. You started as a French major but rapidly ascertained that many of your school's French courses are in 1800's era French literature, something you find as enjoyable as a six year-old finds a plate of broccoli. Along the way, though, you took some classes which afforded you the opportunity to speak French. You do some research and uncover that your school has some business classes that are taught in French. Voila. Now you're a French Business major.

6. Go By the Numbers.

By the time you're a sophomore, especially a second semester sophomore, you've gathered enough information to at least have some choices of majors. The next critical step is to look at the required classes that remain for each of the majors you're considering, and simply mark down which sound good, and which sound terrible. If you see that you need to take nine more classes to be a psychology major, and only two of these seem like they are for you, you now know psychology may not be for you. If six or seven appeal to you, now you're in business.

Honestly, that's kind of it. I recognize, though, that despite everything written here, there will still be tremendous numbers of students (and parents) whose default idea of a "safe" major is business. Here are a few thoughts about this idea:

1. A professor I know is an absolutely brilliant man with incredible insights about how students can make the most of college. He uses the phrase, "It's easier to differentiate than to compete." While this sounds like a saying

written by a hipster for a fortune cookie, it's actually quite poignant. The incredible number of business majors exiting colleges these days means that you are now facing intense job competition from multitudes of peers. Rather than doing what everyone else does, do something different. If you think it's safe and secure to major in business, say, think again: everyone does this, so now you're competing against a horde of people. No one majors in Russian literature anymore. If for some reason you like Dostoevsky, go for it - you'll certainly have something to discuss on a future interview.

2. Certain business majors, like accounting for instance, are clearly necessary for students seeking jobs in that particular field. The vast majority of business-related jobs, however, whether they are in social media or other marketing, management, or other fields, do not require a specific major. Marketing research firms routinely hire psychology majors, as do sales organizations. Even consultants are looking for students with a wide variety of majors.

3. If you major in business of some kind, and you hate it, you're very unlikely to get a lot out of it. I can recall literally only one person ever who succeeded as an entry level employee at my old company who didn't like the work. School is similar; when you don't like something, you spend less time and effort making yourself good at it.

4. Evidence described in a 2012 report suggests that, by students' senior year, those studying in the liberal arts may become better critical thinkers[36] than those majoring in business. Work decisions are often difficult precisely because each time you fix a problem, you create a new situation (and potential problem); critical thinking is precisely the skill required to analyze which potential series of outcomes is most desirable, and why.

5. I majored in marketing and loved it. If you truly have or develop a passion for a business major, of course you should pursue it. Just don't do so thinking it's some kind of job panacea.

---

36 http://cae.org/images/uploads/pdf/Majors_Matter_Differential_Performance_on_a_Test_of_General_College_Outcomes.pdf

6. Mitt Romney. Peter Thiel. Ken Chenault (CEO of Amex, for those who don't know his name). Michael Eisner. Andrea Jung (former CEO of a little company called Avon). Carl Icahn. What do these people have in common, besides spectacular career success? They all majored[37] in liberal arts-type studies.

I'd say good luck with this process (which can be quite stressful), but by following the above, you won't need luck.

Homework

1. Actually look through your high school transcript and circle the three classes you liked the best, irrespective of the teacher.

2. Once college starts, do the exact same thing at the end of each semester.

3. Have a friend read the descriptions of the classes you'd need to take for two different majors, and have them watch your reactions to those classes. Pick the one where they see you cringe less.

37 http://www.businessinsider.com/successful-liberal-arts-majors-2012-12?op=1

CHAPTER 7

Likes to Loves – Translating What You Like Into What You Love and What You Love into Where You Want to Work

"Find your passion" is a phrase many people are fond of saying to college students. But this little homily is often anything but helpful. Most students hear this and think, "Ok great, but how do I do that?" While advice givers mean well here, the end result is more stress, which is the last thing any college student (or anyone) needs.

So how do you find your passion? I like to think of it in the same way you'd think of dating. When you start dating, you realize pretty quickly that you might have a lot in common with one person and nothing to talk about with someone else who you had thought was very alluring. The only way to discover who'd be a better fit for you is to get to know them, and yourself, better.

The same can be said for finding your passion. The best way to go about it is through the sometimes awkward and uncomfortable process of trial and error. When you try a lot of stuff that you think you might like, you'll inevitably discover things that you love, or that turn into something you love.

Below are a few ideas for how to put this theory into practice.

1. Be Like Nike and *Just Do It*

This shopworn phrase still has meaning. *Just do it* is a mantra that any college student can adopt, merely by experimenting with things you think will be interesting. Join a club. Take a cool-sounding class. Volunteer. Volunteering is actually a lot easier than getting a job or internship, but with almost all of the same benefits. Through volunteering, you'll hone in on your interests (the topic of this chapter), learn how to work, gain experience in a particular field and make valuable contacts. All of these are things college students typically lack and are not things people will just "give" you.

Let's say you have thought about coding, but don't have the time or inclination to take a class at school. Use Coursera[38] (or something like it) instead; it's free and online, so you can fit it into your schedule. If you think you might want to be a physician's assistant, volunteer at a hospital. Think you want to be a grade school teacher? Become a Big Brother/Big Sister. Ask your career center for ideas; speak with professors who seem clued in to the community of which you are a part. If it fascinates you, and it's legal, just do it.

2. Speed Date

Speed dating may seem like a super weird concept. Is it dating while high on speed? An interesting idea, but no, speed dating doesn't refer to drugs. Speed dating is a way for people to meet a number of different people and quickly deduce who might be a match. In the context of discovering a passion, you can do the same thing at college. Try a lot of things, then drop those that are not capturing your interest. Give them a real shot, of course, but there's simply no harm in quitting things that are not worthwhile.

3. The Power of Yes.

Yes Man! was a 2008 movie with a powerful point: opportunities occur when you say yes, not when you say no. In the movie, Jim Carrey learns to speak Korean and goes on adventures that he normally wouldn't, if he'd stuck to his old routines. Taking advantage of opportunities and saying yes to possibilities lets you learn that you like giving college tours, playing chess, or dancing in a Bollywood show with 500 of your classmates. Try saying yes when asked to do something and see where it leads you.

---

38 https://www.coursera.org/

4. Patience is Indeed a Virtue.

Another way to attack this issue is to utilize the idea put forth by renowned author Angela Duckworth, who suggests "fostering" your passion,[39] instead of finding it. Amongst the ways she suggests doing so is by being patient and understanding that interests are developed, not discovered. (Check out this book[40] if you want to delve into this topic in great detail.) She asserts, "Don't overthink it. Move in the direction of something that feels better than worse." One point I'd make is that though Ms. Duckworth was discussing this premise in terms of entry-level job seeking, I'd maintain that there's no reason to wait until after you graduate to first foster your passions. Start as a freshman. Don't wait and waste four years.

5. Frequency and Depth Versus Optics

My mantra to all college kids is: do what you like to do, A LOT, and then see what happens. College students often worry about what activities will "look good on a résumé." I read a fantastic quote about this from an MIT volunteer interviewer and Senior Aerospace Engineer, Tom Stagliano: "You can't fake greatness and you can't hide greatness." The takeaway is that a résumé only gets you an interview, not a job; in your interview, when a prospective employer asks you what you did in a club, internship, fellowship, job, voluntary activity or class that you thought was significant enough to mention on your résumé, and your response is essentially, "Um, not that much," you're in worse shape than had you not referenced this activity at all.

Do the stuff that has your interest at the time. If you don't know what that is, try a bunch of things. Then go deep into the few that really capture your attention. That way, when someone asks, you'll be able to answer, without faking it.

---

39 https://www.nytimes.com/2016/06/05/jobs/graduating-and-looking-for-your-passion-just-be-patient.html?_r=0

40 https://books.google.com/books/about/The_Power_of_Interest_for_Motivation_and.html?id=e5j4CgAAQBAJ

Nathan Gebhard puts it another way in this New York Times story,[41] quoting Veronica Belmont,[42] a Web and TV host, producer and writer who has 1.75 million Twitter followers: "If you're really passionate about a topic, and you want to work in that field, you should already be doing it."

Gebhard adds, "Now more than ever, you can glimpse the inner workings of industries. Follow someone on Twitter to gain insight into a field, read industry publications to track trends, or watch free online lectures."

It's not the methods that matter, it's the frequency. If you say you like writing, write. All the time. Write a blog. Write for the school paper. Write for yourself in a notebook. Write poems, short stories, novellas, investigative journalistic pieces, whatever. Just don't say you're a writer, while not actually writing.

6. Uncertainty is Merely Delayed Gratification in Disguise.

Here's a great quote from Paul Graham in a speech [43](Mr. Graham is the founder of Y Combinator, an enormous seed capital firm) that all incoming and existing college students will benefit from, in some way or another. "Work on things that interest you and increase your options, and worry later about which [options] you'll take."

The speech itself is long and replete with thought-provoking ideas. This one, though, struck me as critical, for I think that what often stands in the way of finding the things you really enjoy doing is fear. Trying for a certain outcome often yields a certain outcome, just not the one you expected or wanted. Push through this. You may not be rewarded today, tomorrow or even by semester's end. But you'll be surprised to see after a while how many passions you develop and that the uncertainty you started with actually transforms into gratification.

---

41 https://www.nytimes.com/2015/08/02/education/edlife/four-steps-to-choosing-a-career-path.html?_r=1--nathan

42 http://veronicabelmont.com/

43 http://www.paulgraham.com/hs.html

7. Eye on the Ball.

Remember that after college is over, getting any job is not a goal. Getting a job you might want – that's something to target. If you have the resources to take a job that pays poorly but seems exciting and is moving you on your path, take it. If you need a job that pays, it might still be worth taking a low-paying but exciting gig, provided you can work a second job to pay the bills, live at home to save money, or some combination of the two. Either way, safety and security in your first job are vastly over-rated. Doing a job where you're passionate about your day-to-day tasks, with people you love being around, well, that's nirvana.

And as my very intuitive sister Shelley pointed out, "Working in an exciting job that's low-paying could actually lead to your ultimate higher-paying job. Your passion for that job will show and be rewarded. Conversely, taking that higher-paying, but uninteresting job could backfire in the long-term, as you're less likely to have the drive to thrive and build a career in something you don't like. Employers know when you don't like your job, and you may be left behind when it comes to future promotions."

8. Weaknesses can become strengths.

Not everything you like to do will be something you're initially good at doing. This isn't necessarily a reason to give up so quickly. As a kid, I played basketball for a very brief period of time, and I wasn't particularly talented. I tentatively picked up the game again in my late 20s, then decided to devote myself to improving when I moved to Long Island at age 31, an age when a lot of people are quitting, not starting. Ultimately, I was able to develop enough of a facility for the game to really enjoy it for the next two decades; more meaningfully, I've made an incredible number of close friends through a game, for which I'm grateful every day.

Confidence stems not only from becoming good at something, but also by acknowledging you can get better. [44]"Admitting and working on weaknesses is a great strength. Trying and failing, embracing challenges and risks, these are not bad things. You won't lose every time. With every "win" comes confidence; this

---

44 https://www.nytimes.com/2015/09/13/jobs/playing-the-confidence-game.html

growing confidence will enable you to project your best self to everyone you meet, leading to opportunities you've earned, that are fitting, and that will yield a fulfilling job. And when you devote yourself to your interests, you may just turn them not only into passions, but also into marketable traits. Imagine that.

9. Failing is OK.

Reshma Saujani, Founder and Chief Executive of Girls Who Code, stated in a profound commencement speech, "Make failure part of your narrative and celebrate your rejections, whether you're speaking on a panel, having dinner with friends, or posting on social media. Sharing your failures will help us all stop fearing the 'f word' and to start celebrating it. No one's real life looks the way it does on Instagram."

As you know, the fishbowl effect is very real these days. The problem with no one sharing failures and problems is not only do people feel alone in their troubles, but also that no one gets the help that others can and want to provide.

I ran a successful business for decades and was still messing up stuff in my last week on the job. It's not fun to make mistakes, but it is normal. What's more, it's actually quite illuminating to learn from them.

10. Obsess Much?

Obsessions normally connote something very negative. Turning interests into passions without obsessing at times is probably impossible. According to Drew Houston, CEO of Dropbox a tennis ball is the key to finding a job you love. [45] The tennis ball symbolizes obsession, with Houston averring, "The most successful people ... I know are all obsessed with solving a problem that really matters to them. I use the tennis ball {example} ... because of my dog, who gets this crazy, obsessed look on her face when you throw the ball for her."

For all you college kids and recent graduates, whether on your own or with help, it's time to find your tennis ball.

---

45 https://www.nytimes.com/2016/06/05/business/drew-houston-of-dropbox-figure-out-the-things-you-dont-know.html

11. Introspection is for Winners. Being Too Cool for School, eh, Not So Much.

A dear friend sent me a description of how Bucknell outlines career advice [46]for its students. What leapt off the page for me was this: "[According to] Executive Director of Career Services Pamela Keiser, 'A student is best able to market themselves when they possess a solid understanding of who they are as an individual. This includes their personality, strengths, skills, experiences, and even their gaps or weaknesses, combined with a keen awareness of what their intended career path or industry seeks and expects of candidates when hiring.'"

What great advice. Reiterating a point made earlier, I'd urge you to begin this self-knowledge process on today. Right now. Adjust as you go, always remembering that this isn't a chore, it's a way of later avoiding a job that feels like a chore.

12. Satisfaction Can Yield Cash

Money or happiness? The great debate, and a question that college students and recent college graduates add to their list of things to ponder, things most likely to make them even more anxious. But why not both? For decades I've been telling people that it's better to feel fulfilled at work, which then leads to happiness, which often leads to increased pay as well.

Experts are quantifying this. In relation to really immersing yourself in something you enjoy Robert Frank, a Cornell Economics professor, stated, " .... becoming an expert is so challenging that you are unlikely to expend the necessary effort unless the task is one that you love for its own sake. If it is, the process will be rewarding apart from whether it leads to high pay."[47]

Absolutely true, and wonderfully poignant. He goes on to say:

---

46 http://bucknellian.net/61036/features/from-campus-to-cubicle-how-you-can-garner-career-worthy-skills-in-college/

47 https://www.nytimes.com/2016/07/24/upshot/first-rule-of-the-job-hunt-find-something-you-love-to-do.html?_r=0

"The happiness literature has identified one of the most deeply satisfying human psychological states to be one called 'flow.' It occurs when you are so immersed in an activity that you lose track of the passage of time. If you can land a job that enables you to experience substantial periods of flow, you will be among the most fortunate people on the planet. What's more, as the years pass, you will almost surely develop deep expertise at whatever it is you've been doing. At that point, even if few people in any one location place high value on what you do, *you may find that your services become extremely valuable economically.*" (Italics were added here for emphasis.)

There you have it.

13. Don't Listen to Haters.

As you begin to pursue your interests and develop strengths, people will ask why you're "wasting time" on *that*, with the "that" being something of which they disapprove or in which they see no value. My dear family friend and future SNL star Addie Ronis, speaking recently at her high school graduation, shared this incredibly insightful tidbit:

"Embrace your strengths and throw them at people who say they don't matter."

This reminded of a quote from former champion bodybuilder and later California Governor Arnold Schwarzenegger. When people said to him, "We never want to look like you," he replied, "Don't worry, because you never will."

Other people will never know you as well as you know yourself. Pursuing the tenets suggested above will make you confident and competent, whereas listening to people who don't take the time to find out who you really are will fill you with self-doubt. Ignore them.

College is a place to develop competence to match your passions. When you do, fulfillment will follow.

Homework

1. Go to your career center, explain that you want to volunteer in your neighborhood, and review the choices they present. Pick one and start.

2. Join a club that is similar to classes you've enjoyed. Ask other students in that club what they're doing for the summer, and then mimic the jobs they're holding if they're in your field of interest.

3. Athletes: try out for a play. Musicians: join an intramural team. Finance majors: become active in student government. Try anything to discover a new interest, even if you're bad at it.

CHAPTER 8

Clubs

One of the starkest differences I see in college campuses today than in "the old days" is the push for students to join clubs. I was a member of the Marketing Society, but I cannot recall the reason I joined and it wasn't like we had tons of members. That said, I made three close friends in that club who are still an important part of my life; none of them lived in my dorm, and two didn't even live on the same campus as I did. We knew one another from class, but that club is where we got to know each other better.

I also played a lot of intramurals, and similarly made some lasting friends. Additionally, I really enjoyed spending time with a bunch of these guys outside of playing ball, and through one of the teams I met a bunch of older kids with whom I'd otherwise never have connected.

When I think back on this, though, I realize that my experience was somewhat unusual; when I speak with people with whom I went to college, no one remembers the school or other kids pressing us freshmen to join clubs. If you were interested in something, and you happened to notice it, that was fine. If not, no one was bringing your attention to it.

Now, that's not the case at all. Every tour you go on at every school stresses the amount and variability of the clubs the school offers; many even end by saying something like, "And if you don't see a club that interests you, start one."

Besides air-conditioned dorm rooms, which simply didn't exist way back when, the emphasis on clubs is one of the greatest improvements for students that colleges have made over the years. I don't say that lightly, either. Here are a few reasons why, listed in order of what I think are most to least important:

1. ***Meet a Lot More People.***

As mentioned above, being in clubs is an incredibly natural way of making friends. First and foremost, you're interacting with people who share your interests, which is an automatic "ice breaker" and a far easier way to meet people than forced trust builder exercises. I loved playing baseball, which morphed into softball, which led me to a team of older kids who had met me briefly in our dorm. From there, I met their friends, guys they had known for a few years, and before long this meant I had a new friend group to hang with if other kids from my dorm weren't around (or even if they were). The best part is they were unlike other kids I met; a bunch of them were a lot smarter than I was, and they talked about incredibly complicated things. Of course they also spent most of their time making fun of one another, and taught me how to do a "dine and dash," so that was nice.

One of the most effective means of immersing yourself in college, and consequently eliminating homesickness, loneliness and a host of other negative 'nesses, is to make a lot of friends. For many students, though, this translates to identifying and latching onto a select group of kids who are exactly like them. Everyone understands the appeal of replacing your high school friend group immediately at college. The downside? You miss out on a plethora of amazing people by limiting yourself to finding kids exactly like you, kids who share your religion and your socioeconomic sphere and even the county where you're from. It's a little like ordering a burger at every restaurant on a tour of 10 European countries; sure, they'll likely be fine, but the way you discover that octopus is amazing is by trying it. (My vegetarian/vegan friends are encouraged, sort of, to substitute kale over iceberg in this metaphor.)

The other piece of this is that different clubs will attract different kinds of people. When you think of your interests, are they ever the exact same as everyone in your high school friend group? Or even of anyone you know? When you play Frisbee golf, you'll meet kids who like doing that. This holds true for debate, student government, entrepreneurial stuff, dance, art, etc. None of the kids in each of these clubs will be in all of them, which means you'll naturally expand the amount of friend groups you have. Additionally, you'll enjoy the friends of friends phenomenon I mentioned above, where it's possible and even likely that you'll end up becoming better friends with people who started as merely friends of your friends than you remain with the original friend. In any case, you sure as shit won't be lonely ever again.

2. *Prepare Yourself for the Job World*

Spoiler alert: Sylvester Stallone will still be making Rocky sequels even after you graduate. Spoiler alert 2: When you get a real job after college, there is a 100% chance that there's a zero % chance that you'll be working with a group of people who are exactly like you. No, you'll be working with people of all ages, genders, stripes and religions. People with different political views. People with mortgages, kids and obligations, obligations that cause them tremendous stress. People who won't put up with someone who's thin-skinned, or who plays on their phone during a meeting, or who lets others do their work in a group project. This is the so-called real world, something you want to start preparing yourself for. The good news is you have four years of incredible safety, four years where you can explore and learn but where many of you aren't thinking about finances. Like the Green Lantern's energy bubble, this is a great thing to have, but it's not permanent. While you have it, use it. Join clubs that allow you, even force you, to deal with kids who aren't the same as you. Even if you don't love all of them, you'll learn a lot about group dynamics, how you behave in a group, and even how to influence a group. You will never learn any of this by exclusively hanging out with the same five people you met in your frat freshman year.

Even if the pull of safety is so great that you need to have your friend group solidified on Day 2 of college, don't limit yourself to this group for four years. There is no chance when you graduate you'll work with a group of people just like you, and at the risk of sounding like a nag, you'll be incredibly ill-suited to work with people different than you if you've never been at least friends with them before.

3. *Uncover Your Passions and Identify Possible Majors*

A benefit of clubs that few people discuss is that clubs can help solidify your interests, and conversely, help you identify those areas that it turns out don't really captivate you any longer. Let's say that in high school you were in student government, took A.P. Government, and spent a lot of time talking about government. Naturally in college you join student government, and start taking some government-related classes. After a semester or two, it dawns on you that while you like aspects of government, you don't want to major in it, and you sure don't want to work in it following school. Has your time exploring this been a "waste?" Absolutely not. As you'll recall from the previous chapter, the very best outcome for every student is learning what things they like might actually be things they love. Participating actively in multiple clubs speeds up this self-knowledge and therefore is an extraordinarily beneficial process to undertake. The experiences you have, both in and out of the classroom, are key aids in helping you define your future paths.

4. *Content*

I put content last for a reason: I don't think it matters. Sure, you'll want to join stuff that interests you. That's obvious. Equally clear is that if you determine you no longer care for something, or the club just sucks, you can quit, and try something else. There's no penalty for this. Beyond that, though, it really doesn't matter what type of club(s) you join, as long as you join some, for the other three reasons explicated above.

I know there are some people quietly shaking their heads and thinking, "yeah, but don't you want/need to have certain clubs to make your résumé stand out?" I'll answer that question with one of my own: "Do you know of an employer in a non-scientific field that cares about what clubs a student has joined?" I'll move onto the next chapter while you write your list.

Homework

1. Join something you've never done before, like student radio.

2. Try a new club at least once a year, and preferably one a semester.

3. Make a goal to meet one friend from each club you join.

CHAPTER 9

How to Meet Professors, and Why You Should

C olleges offer a wealth of resources that you as a student pay for, without always realizing it. Sadly, an often under-utilized resource is interaction with professors. I'll explain why, but more notably, I'll present some ideas on how to address this issue, and generate incredible benefits in the process.

Why don't students approach their professors?

A common belief among incoming college students is that being a "teacher's pet," a typically unwanted position, is the natural and even the only outgrowth of forming relationships with teachers. While this may have some credence in high school, in college it is simply ridiculous. College students are so focused on themselves and their own work burdens that paying attention to other students approaching a professor isn't at all a concern. Beyond that, professors have office hours that guarantee privacy of the interaction. Finally, college is an expensive venture, and thus taking advantage of the things one is paying for is not only a good idea, but is absolutely necessary for success.

The larger reason for failing to form relationships with professors is fear. Many students are nervous about being rebuffed, aren't sure when or who to approach, and simply don't know what to say to start the relationship. I'll address each of these in turn.

Fear of rejection

The fear of rejection is almost completely unfounded.

While not every professor is interested in conversing with students, many are. In fact, many got into this line of work precisely to interact with smart young people.

Numerous professors will say that they wish they were being approached more often, not less. In fact, students who update a professors years later with what the student has been doing will make a professor's whole day. My aforementioned friend Eric Kriftcher put it really well, "Most professors really want to help; many love creating a lasting legacy by paying it forward to future generations. Give them the opportunity to do that."

Who to Approach, and When

The first part of this answer is remarkably simple: start with the professors, or even the TA's (teacher's assistants) who you like. The professors who seem most engaging in class will be the easiest to approach after class.

A note here regarding ratemyprofessor.com, a website where students, as the name implies, rate professors. While this can be an incredible resource, use caution here. Think of this like asking a waiter to bring you his favorite dish. Since you have no idea what this person's tastes are, the fact that they bring food from the kitchen to customers yields very little real data for you. Instead, telling the waiter that you love spicy food and asking for the spiciest dish on the menu gives you a far better likelihood that you'll enjoy your meal. Use ratemyprofessor.com similarly. Look for the criteria you care about in a teacher rather than simple ratings. Read detailed descriptions about why someone else didn't like something about a professor, which turn out to be the very thing you enjoy. If a professor is notable for being someone who engages the class in discussions rather than lecturing, a person who would rather participate would view this trait positively. If this is you, this professor would be great; who cares if others rate him poorly?

As for when to start the dialogue, multiple, simple methods exist. Email. Drop in during open office-hours. Or go to the professor's public Google calendar. Once a relationship is developed, additional forms of communication will present themselves.

What Do I Say?

Here are a few ideas:

1. Start small and specific.
    a. Speak about a particular point the professor made in a recent class that you found stimulating.
    b. Ask how the professor became interested in the course being taught; actually listen to the answer, which often will be quite illuminating.

2. Ask things that are not time sensitive and that a professor can answer; don't put the professor in a position to fail you. Ask a marketing professor to comment on the name of the new club or company you are about to start. Don't ask them to review your business plan.

3. If you love the class, but it is outside of your major, ask your professor about related on-campus activities and clubs that you can join. My sister related the following, "In college, I took a marketing class outside of my major. After a presentation I had done, my professor asked me if I was in the marketing club, to which I replied that I was not, was not a marketing major or even a business major, and that I didn't know anything about it. He strongly recommended that I join the club anyway, but I asked no questions and basically dismissed his idea, assuming that he knew nothing about me. Later in life, I realized that I should have been more open-minded and talked to him about the club and whatever general insights he would offer me about the field of marketing. Oddly enough, although I didn't see it then, I did end up in a field related to marketing, totally outside of my major. I could have moved onto that path much quicker had I even had a short conversation with that professor."

The above-referenced Ian Bullard, one of my first mentees and an obviously budding star, explained a psychological theory which states, essentially, that when you ask someone for a small, discrete favor or opinion, while offering them nothing in return, somehow that person then develops an affinity for you. It seems peculiar, but evidently it's accurate. Eventually this series of interactions will lead to deeper relationships where you can ask for bigger things, or where you will be asked to do bigger things. (Ian had a professor literally offer him a summer job, out of nowhere, in a short chat where Ian was merely discussing an internship he was thinking was not a good fit.) These relationships are quite different than the superficial "we connected on LinkedIn but then I never reached out in any other way" relationships many kids "develop" with their professors (and other adults). I'd even argue that the latter relationships are offensive to most adults who view them, correctly, as a waste of their time.

What Else Should I Know?

1. Brevity is good. As alluded to above, it's ok if your initial interactions with professors are brief. Remember, your goal is to develop a genuine, lasting relationship, which by definition takes time; you are not here for "résumé-building." Do not ask about a grade or a test; this will not distinguish you and will not lead to further conversations.

2. Set goals. Promise that you'll meet one professor per semester, and you'll be amazed how your college experience is transformed.

3. Understand that not all professors will respond, and some will answer so late that the question you had was long since answered. Adjust your questions and your expectations, accordingly. And like in sales, you may have to reach out to 10 professors to form meaningful connections with four of them. As an ancillary benefit, the rejection will help you form a thick skin, which will prove quite useful as you begin interviewing for jobs at some point.

4. The deeper the relationship the better. This holds true for future references the professor may provide for you, as well as for every other benefit that accrues from authentic and long-lasting interactions. Start cultivating these relationships early.

It bears repeating that many professors are eager to interact with students. Take them up on it. You will never be sorry that you did this, but you'll definitely regret not doing so.

Homework

1. Get to really know one professor every semester.

2. Have coffee with each member of your professor crew once a semester.

3. Read this.[48]

---

48 https://medium.com/@lportwoodstacer/how-to-email-your-professor-without-being-annoying-af-cf64ae0e4087#.m27jizdx5

CHAPTER 10

Building a Network

I t's not what you know; it's who you know. How many times have you heard that phrase? Leaving aside the privilege issues (these are important but are best laid out in another book), the problem with this premise is that people believe their network is fixed somehow, that "who you know" has more to do with your parents' jobs than any active measures you might take.

This is bullshit. Obviously, taking advantage of any connections your parents might have is a smart idea. But thinking this will either be a panacea (it won't) or that it won't help at all (also not true) stops most people from building their own network. Your parents are not you; often times their connections are limited to the fields in which they have spent their careers, which may not overlap with the career you are looking to forge.

One of the most important lessons for college students (and for us parents as well) centers on the idea that students can and indeed, must build their own networks. Doing so will make you more independent, more confident, and more successful in the ultimate end game of college, i.e., the job search. Developing your own network is like learning how to drive, to cook an egg, or to do laundry.

Building a network is a little like building a house. Unless you know of a miraculous way to erect a house all in one shot, doing so requires multiple steps. Unlike building a house, however, network building is not linear; it's not as if each step requires waiting for the previous one to be completed. You can and will meet multiple people in all walks of your life, simultaneously and continuously.

By now many of you are thinking, "Shit, this sounds awful. I hope my parents' friends just hook me up with a job." I don't blame you. Networking the traditional way sucks, and sadly, doesn't even work. [49] When you treat networking like a game

---

49 https://www.fastcompany.com/3059070/your-most-productive-self/8-common-networking-disasters-and-how-to-avoid-them

where the winner is the person who has the most nonsensical, short conversations with people whose names you've forgotten before they've walked away, results will be poor.

But networking doesn't have to be like this at all. What if instead you considered all of your every-day relationships as networking, instead of going to awkward meet and greet networking functions at which the highlight is the mini hot dog in the Pillsbury dough? How would this change anything? Simple: when you actively engage with people you meet, from fellow students and their parents to professors and your parents' friends, they'll remember you and think highly of you. Later, when you ask for a favor, they may actually do it.

Below are a few specific (and free) techniques for accomplishing this. Choose whichever ones appeal to you:

1. **Talk to People**.

   My family was doing a vacation hike in a pretty remote spot and came across another family doing the same thing. We could hear the father's French accent (my older son speaks French), and saw the older daughter had shorts showing she goes to the same school as my older son. Speaking to them, we learned they also come from NYC. Three odd coincidences, leading to one very cool interaction. Will this result in a job for my son one day? How the hell do I know? But neither does he, and so speaking with these people, and adding them to your network, can never hurt. And one day it might just help. A lot.

2. **When You Talk, Care.**

   You're introduced to your roommate's dad during visiting day. When you ask him a question, actually care about the answers. This will force you to ask only those questions that interest you, and whose answers you'll remember. You'll want to follow up, because you'll be curious about the result of whatever you were discussing. In turn, your roomie's pop will think of you as a friend, instead of someone he vaguely knows. When I meet someone new, whether it's at a party, a bar or at work, I'm always fascinated by why that person chose whatever field in which he works, so I'll often ask this question. Additional questions easily emerge depending on the reply. And when I see that person again, we now have a topic to discuss.

3. **Spin.**

When people ask you what you're majoring in, responding, "I dunno" isn't helpful. You've provided the questioner no information, and dialogue ceases. "I've really been enjoying my history and philosophy classes, so I'm looking into possibly majoring in one of those," on the other hand, will spark a discussion that could take in you any number of directions.

Tell your story with a spin focusing on what you like the most. One of my first and most receptive mentees, Katie Gennusa, had a strong interest in working in fashion, but had been dissuaded from it by both adults and peers. When we chatted about this, it emerged that Katie was expressing her interest in a way that was harming her. We altered the message from, "I'm thinking of working in retail," which sounded like she wanted to be a shirt folder at the Gap, to "I've loved working at a boutique, as I've gotten a chance to design the store window, I've designed store themes, and I even went to NYC to select merchandise." The latter story was received very positively and left her feeling confident that her decision to seek a job in this field was the right move. After college, she indeed landed an assistant buyer post at TJ Maxx, an enormous, well-known firm.

4. **Put Yourself Out There**.

A family friend of mine was at the theater with her mom, who happened to chat with the person sitting next to her. Somehow the conversation turned to writing, which my friend is into; it turned out the seat neighbor knew a famous restauranteur who was starting a new kind of food business and who was looking for a food blogger. Bingo. My friend presented herself to the founder as a foodie who could write, and just like that got herself a summer gig at a job she had no idea existed prior to this exchange.

5. **Don't Ask What Google Can Easily Answer.**

One aspect of networking involves what to ask of the person with whom you're speaking. One way of garnering a useful response is to ask the other person for their opinions and impressions, rather than for what I'd call researchable facts.

You are intrigued by nutrition; question a nutritionist on the classes they'd suggest you take and the various opportunities that exist in that field. Ask about whether they work directly with customers as part of a clinical, or whether they setting broad policy in an institutional setting. Find out the differences between these positions. And if you must, ask why a salad is better for you than a Big Mac. Just don't ask them what colleges have nutrition programs; this they probably don't know, and moreover, you can find out by Googling.

6. **LinkedIn is for Peers, Not Just for Adults.**

Students think of LinkedIn as a place solely to connect with adults. But as pointed out by a very astute mentee of mine, Jacob Heifetz-Licht, you also should use LinkedIn to connect to other students. Suppose you and another student, especially an older one from your school, are both working a summer internship in NYC. Reaching out on LinkedIn can be an effective means of setting up a meeting, where you can ask for any advice they may have for you. If you're interested in computer science, for example, who better than someone a few years older to explain how to gain practical experience versus classroom experience?

7. **Networking is Two-way.**

As stated in our chapter on meeting professors, asking for tiny favors and offering nothing in return other than gratitude can be very appealing to the person who's helping you, even if this seems somewhat counter-intuitive. Still, the best relationships are those where both parties help one another. Admittedly, you may have less to offer an adult at the onset. But as time goes on, this will change. If nothing is obvious, ask what you can do to help the other person. Even if the answer is nothing, the gesture, if genuine, will be greatly appreciated. Be observant, and offer to help in an area where you're more talented than the adult. I've had mentees help re-write my materials, make suggestions for my website, and write and post flyers on their campuses, all at their request. There's even a term for this: reverse mentoring.[50]

---

50 http://host.madison.com/wsj/business/mentoring-has-evolved-to-become-knowledge-sharing/article_8c735d68-50fa-5410-abd6-7a6d0129634b.html

Few things are more heart-warming than doing good deeds for people who do good deeds for you.

8. **Networking isn't Just a Job Hunt.**

Sure, the eventual goal of developing a network is to help you in a job quest. But approaching your relationships like you'd approach an Easter egg hunt will be ineffective. Most adults aren't stupid; if you are transparently interested only in what job they can get for you at that moment, the likelihood of them spending a lot of time helping you is slim. Treat each relationship as a reward in and of itself. Become a person the other person really cares about. Talk about your classes, your part-time jobs, and other things going on in your life, and ask about theirs. Then trust that when the time is right, they'll introduce you to someone who might have a need for your skills.

9. **Six Degrees of Separation.**

A common theory students have is that none of the adults they've met, or who are friends of their parents, have any connection to whatever field that interests the student. This assumes that whatever little box each person inhabits is their whole universe. The problem with this theory is that it is absurd; because people abide by it, though, they lose out on legions of opportunities that are created by asking your network *who they know*. A friend's son wanted a summer research position but didn't know that a friend's dad's best friend had just such an opening to fill. After speaking to her family at Thanksgiving about the job she was seeking, a mentee of mine learned that her brother's friend's mom coincidentally worked at one of the companies on her list. I gave a speech and mentioned, as an aside, my friendship with a well-respected sports journalist. In the audience was a student who deeply admired that journalist, and was overwhelmed at the thought of having the opportunity to speak with him. This never would have happened if the student didn't approach me after the speech and mention his esteem for my friend. Instead of assuming, therefore, talk to everyone you know about what you're looking to do, what interests you and what you're up to now. Then ask what they think. I guarantee that at least one person, and probably many, will surprise you by announcing that they know other people who can help.

10. **Adults Love Dispensing Advice.**

Students have the nagging capacity to forget that adults were once exactly like them. Sure, it might have been decades earlier, and the world unquestionably has changed since then. But no adult forgets their own experiences as a nervous teenager, and almost all adults are more than willing to help someone in their circle. In fact, I'd argue that most adults derive significant pleasure and pride by doing just that; helping a younger person is an energizing feeling that is proven to help adults feel younger. You're not "bothering" someone by asking for advice or assistance. These relationships, if handled using the techniques outlined above, are quite symbiotic.

11. **The More the Merrier, As People Say.**

James Altucher, an entrepreneur, well-known podcaster and author (of amongst other things, a book entitled "How to Become a Master at Networking"), shared the following post on "How to Make a Lot of Money." (I'll stress again that I don't subscribe to the theory that making a lot of money should be an end goal. That said, there's some excellent information about networking in this post, so I'm including it all.)

"Here is all the advice I've gotten in the past few days. I collect advice and try to figure out what to do with it later.

1. 'If you want to make a million dollars, help a million people.'

2. 'If you want to make a million, go for ten million.'

3. 'Get up early, so you have an extra hour each day over your competition.'

"This is all decent advice. I don't know. I've never done any of it. BUT, I can tell you what is common among all the people who gave me the advice. Their network of contacts is huge. They stay in touch with hundreds of people and then when the time is right, they know how to put the right people together and they get a cut in the middle. Sometimes the cut is a million dollars or more.

I try to add one person to my network every day. Maybe today I will add you."

12. Write Thank You Cards.

You say corny, I say memorable. I've received some beautiful and thoughtful thank you cards from people I've mentored, including the aforementioned Katie Gennusa and Madeleine Thornburn; for all of you who think this kind of thing doesn't matter, or is silly, or will take too long, you're wrong. There's something very powerful about a hand-written card, something that says you actually care enough to take a little time to express your thoughts in a super personal way.

Homework

1. Get started today. Remember, networking starts day one of college.

2. If you're a sophomore, junior or senior, think back to the people you've met, and start making deeper connections. Invite a professor to coffee, and ask why they got interested in their field. Ask your dad's funny friend to breakfast, and pepper him with questions about his day to day work life. Take notes about which things interest you, and which don't.

3. If you treat networking like a game with a clear winner, you'll lose. Think of it instead as expanding your friend group, just not with people who'll care about what you post on Snapchat. Look at your LinkedIn page, and set a goal of doubling your contacts. Then write all of them inmails describing what you want to do, and for any advice they might have.

4. Follow up every time you meet someone. I attended a networking-oriented dinner at Rutgers, run by a group of very engaged, mostly business focused students. Each adult was at a table with seven or so students. After three hours of stimulating conversation, after I handed out my business card and specifically stated that I had further information and ideas to share, I was contacted by only one student. If you're choosing to go to events like this,

follow up. Whenever you meet someone with whom you feel any sort of connection, follow up. Make a relationship. I understand that it's tempting to talk yourself out of doing so, because it seems intimidating. When I was 12, I had a paper route. I had to collect money from my customers; if they didn't pay, I could actually lose money. Knocking on doors and seeking to be paid was nerve-wracking at first. After a while, however, it became normal. Start your collections today.

CHAPTER 11

Getting a Mentor, or Mentors

The benefits of mentors for college students are undeniable and well documented, as discussed in the Introduction to this book. For those who still have doubts about the efficacy of mentors, LinkedIn's series on mentorship[51] makes some fascinating points, as told by people you'll recognize. I'm often asked why college students need a mentor, with the hidden or not so hidden subtext being that they should "learn things on their own." The LinkedIn series answer: "When questioned about their career trajectories, you'll find that most successful entrepreneurs credit a mentor or mentors. **No one learns in a vacuum, and it's the men and women who are able to sponge up the wisdom of others .... who set themselves apart**." (Boldness added by me for effect. And because I like bolding things.)

According to a 2015 Gallup poll,[52] recent graduates who strongly agree with *any* of the following three items "are almost twice as likely to strongly agree that their education was worth the cost:"

1. Having professors who cared about them as a person.

2. Having a mentor who encouraged them to pursue their goals and dreams

   Or

3. Having at least one professor who made them excited about learning.

---

51 https://www.entrepreneur.com/slideshow/249233

52 http://www.gallup.com/opinion/gallup/185942/gallup-purdue-index-2015-report-available.aspx

The poll added, "These relationships hold even when controlling for personality characteristics and other variables such as student loan debt and employment status that could also be related to graduates' perceptions that college was worth it."

This echoed themes revealed in a previous Gallup-Purdue index,[53] which was developed through interviews with 30,000 college graduates.

Belle B. Cooper, an iOS developer, writer and a co-founder of Hello Code,[54] a Melbourne-based startup, averred in a blog post, "I haven't found a type of learning that increases my knowledge and improves my skills and output as quickly as mentorship. Having someone around who can answer my questions and help me fix my mistakes[55] is an invaluable resource."

As for someone closer to the age of my college readers, Adam Ibrahim, a 2014 Binghamton graduate and now on his way to becoming a real estate kingpin there, asserted, "It is essential for students to have mentors who they admire, who are not their parents, who support them and offer guidance and positive characteristics to emulate and embody."

Now that that's settled, we can move on to the process of picking the right mentors, people who can bring out the best in you even when you don't know what your best is.

When You Should Get a Mentor

A good mentor will be of benefit to you as soon as you start college. Parents may forget how long and difficult a journey it was for most adults to carve out a professional niche, and that is for the few who actually have been so fortunate. Dissecting ourselves and building our core skill set is something that almost always takes years. Starting earlier creates exponential advantages.

Who Can Be Your Mentors?

The reason I keep using the plural here is that students can have multiple mentors, depending on the mentors' skills and time commitments. A combination of college resources, including academic advisors, professors, department heads and older students (as discussed in Chapter 4), along with bosses and outside adults (professional mentors/coaches, entrepreneurs, industry-specific professionals) can be ideal. While

53 https://www.nytimes.com/2015/09/13/opinion/sunday/frank-bruni-how-to-measure-a-colleges-value.html

54 http://hellocode.co/

55 http://plan.io/blog/post/150350285058/a-short-guide-to-mentoring-why-its-useful-why

the responsibility for navigating these relationships ultimately falls on you, an efficient outside mentor will both encourage these auxiliary relationships and help you facilitate them by acting as a sort-of Dean of Mentors.

I'll discuss below the qualities a true mentor needs to have; meanwhile, I'd stress that merely being called an advisor doesn't make someone a person who'll give you good advice. As an over-arching theme, a mentor is only a mentor if they truly get to know you as an individual, with all your likes, dislikes, strengths, quirks and even insecurities. Someone who calls themselves an advisor (or a mentor) but who can't identify your favorite sport, food or class you've taken is an advisor in name only.

How to Select a Mentor

Finding a mentor, or mentors, is not difficult, though finding the right ones can certainly be far more challenging. Colleges routinely highlight, both in discussions as well as in articles and on their own websites, that they provide students with academic and professional advisors. Students, conversely, present an entirely different story, with almost all of those I've met declaring that while academic counseling is certainly present, the "advice" and guidance they receive from career counseling offices is practically or utterly zero. This is hardly surprising, given the ratio of students to counselors at even small schools; how can each counselor reasonably be expected to really get to know many hundreds of students, enough to understand each student's skills, motivations, interests and possible career paths?

Naturally I believe very strongly in what my company does to supplement what colleges themselves provide. But this book isn't an advertisement for my firm[56] (couldn't help this brief plug – forgive me). With that said, let's focus on the kinds of qualities you'll want your mentors to have.

1. **Time**

   I put this as the number one item for a reason: any mentor who doesn't have enough time to provide you with personalized attention is not a mentor. It's that simple. I don't mean to suggest that a mentor is at your service 24 hours a day, like a concierge at a fancy hotel. But neither is a person who offers to let you

---

56 http://www.oneononementors.com/

"shadow" them at work once for a few hours a true mentor. This is a useful exercise, for sure, but a mentor/mentee relationship takes real time to develop for it to flourish. This is particularly true because you'll change your focus as your time at school evolves, even if your job sights miraculously stay exactly the same. A good mentor will guide you through all the phases of school, from selecting classes freshman year through interviewing for jobs as a soon-to-be graduate. This cannot happen without each of you dedicating a significant block of time.

Older students, or peer mentors, can struggle with this, as they have their own college life to experience. Older students frequently are extremely valuable sources of information, but don't be disappointed when they can't devote as much time to you as you might like.

2. Trustworthiness

The last thing you need in a mentor is a blabbermouth. Effective mentoring means sometimes hearing things that students don't want other people knowing. The number one rule for mentors is to only relate to others that which a student has approved. (Note that a mentor is not a therapist, and will explain to a student who might be in trouble that other professionals need to be contacted, should such a situation arise.)

3. Non-judgmental

This quality speaks for itself but needs to be emphasized anyway. One of the reasons students relate well to mentors is that mentors are not their parents. Even perfect parents, should they exist, cannot escape nature; most kids want and need to separate from their parents at some point, leading to a period where parents may be considered idiots. Other adults do not invite such scrutiny, and thus are in a position to say things to students (even, at times, the exact same thing a parent might say) and have the student listen. This ONLY works, however, if the mentor is non-judgmental; for the second a mentor becomes judgmental, his credibility with the student is shot.

A mentor should explain **why** you should do something, and especially **how** you should do it. A mentor shouldn't be telling you **what** to do.

4. Seasoning/Listening Ability

As discussed here, "An ideal mentor is someone who is either aligned with your goals or has enough experience to help you achieve them. ..." Professors, especially those who've worked in your chosen field or better, continue to do so, are perfect candidates for being mentors. Your boss at an internship or a volunteer position is likewise in a position to offer specific steps for you to take to maximize your time in school. If you have dreams of being an entrepreneur, speaking with someone who's founded and run companies can be ideal. A career services person who meets with you for 15 minutes every third Tuesday and who has never worked outside academia? I'll let you decide on that one.

Of course, none of this matters if the mentor isn't able to get you to explicate your goals, which won't happen if the mentor always does all the talking. One of my first mentees mentioned to me that her previous mentors had shared this disturbing tendency to talk at her, rather than to listen to her. You can imagine this didn't produce such positive results. Good listening flows from caring, something a mentor can't fake. If they don't really care about you, you'll be able to tell, and you should move on accordingly.

5. A Spine.

As the relationship deepens, you'll want a mentor who can challenge you, aiding you in your quest to realize your full potential. This requires a certain degree of toughness on the mentor's part, and on yours. Asking for advice, then implementing it, isn't the same as asking someone else to do something for you, and is a heck of a lot better than giving up. But asking for advice and implementing it can be difficult, if it means changing behaviors you've become accustomed to. A true mentor will make this process as smooth as it can be, while not allowing you to coast either.

6. A Great Memory. Or a Notebook.

Few things are more irksome than opening up to someone who then asks the same questions the next time you meet. A good mentor must keep track of your conversations, texts, emails and meetings; unless the mentor is an elephant, you'll want them to take notes, as corny as this may seem. This will also be a very telling method of examining whether school officials are really mentoring you, or whether you are as anonymous to them as the newspaper delivery man is to a suburban homeowner.

7. Organized.

The last thing you need is a disorganized mentor. It's enough that many college students themselves are either somewhat disorganized or just need to make frequent schedule changes due to the nature of college. Add a mentor who's either disorganized or forever cancelling appointments and you're left with a relationship that's as useful as a hockey stick to a turtle.

8. Entertaining.

A mentor doesn't have to be Eric Andre of Louie C.K., but neither should a mentor be a complete dud either. Part of the process of drawing out the best in a younger person is making that process seem less like work and more like a natural conversation two people would have. Without some element of humor, this can be very difficult to sustain.

9. Clear-headed.

Mentors provide value by helping students break down complex situations and come to tactical and reachable solutions. A good mentor will focus on small steps you can take instead of bombarding you with overly broad and difficult "assignments."

10. In Your Field ....Or Not.

If a mentor happens to be in your field of interest, fantastic. But mentors don't need to be doing exactly what you think you want to do to be effective. In fact, many mentors are valuable precisely because they offer different perspectives and insight stemming from a wide variety of experience. Any mentor with the qualities cited above will help you develop applicable skills regardless of the line of work you ultimately enter.

Finally, as with classes, clubs, jobs and volunteer assignments, mediocre mentors are fungible. You certainly owe the relationship a real chance to thrive, but if it doesn't after a reasonable amount of time, punt and move on to another person. This is a relationship that like the others mentioned, is worth pursuing only when each party is getting something positive out of it.

Homework

1. Approach your most compelling professor during office hours with a question or a thought about something you heard in class. Keep doing this throughout the semester; develop and test the relations using the above parameters.

2. During a slow period, ask your boss how he got into his line of work.

3. Invite your parents' most engaging friend for breakfast on your break. Yep – get up early, as this friend will have to go to work. Ask this person about their job now, jobs they had before, what they've learned from good bosses and bad ones, and anything else that emerges. Focus on being interested, not being interesting.

CHAPTER 12

During School: Do I Get a Job? An Internship? Volunteer?

Wow. There's so much to discuss here it's hard to know where to begin. From the vast changes in your needs and abilities that will occur from freshman year through senior year, to the distinctions between jobs (during the school and over the summers), internships (paid and not paid) and volunteering opportunities, as well as the way you'll want to act on a job, this chapter has a lot to cover. Let's get to it.

Goals

By now you've observed that I'm preachy about setting goals; I firmly believe that doing so is by far the best way of ensuring that you get out of college everything you possibly can, and avoid being this guy.[57]

As mentioned above, your needs and abilities obviously will change as you progress through school. Ipso facto, your goals will change as well. Perhaps a timeline will help elucidate this:

---

57 https://www.google.com/search?hl=en&site=imghp&tbm=isch&source=hp&biw=1280&bih=557& q=no+ragrets+tattoo&oq=no+ragrets&gs_l=img.1.1.0l10.857.2193.0.3565.10.7.0.3.3.0.98.495.6.6.0....0...1 ac.1.64.img..1.9.517.FQLnq1DUdU8#imgrc=oqKSM9NjghZg5M%3A

Before College

An otherwise depressing article about how teenagers are working at far lower rates[58] than in years past claims "Research[59] shows that for every year teenagers work while in high school, income rises an average of 15 percent when they are in their 20s." Enough said.

Freshman Year, First Semester

Many students enter college thinking that they should get a job right away. And colleges often offer plenty of on-campus opportunities to work, which removes one of the major obstacles you'll face in subsequent years.

The questions, as always, are what's motivating the desire to work, and what the costs of doing so are.

1. Money

   No one knows your financial situation better than you do. Except your parents/guardians, who absolutely know more about this, and who you should be consulting before you decide you "need" money. What exactly do you need the money for? Pocket cash for hanging out? Paying college bills? A close friend told me upon recently entering college that she definitely needed a job. A conversation with her mother revealed that this friend had saved more than $10,000 already, and that her parents were paying for college entirely. While wanting to work is an admirable trait, in this instance saying she "needed the money" wasn't particularly accurate (I won't delve into the psychological reasons that might be the wellspring for this need, as I'm not a psychologist).

   What is the cost of working in your first semester of college? As you'll learn if you take Microeconomics 101, the concept of opportunity cost is what's critical to grasp. Essentially, opportunity cost measures the cost of what you give up by choosing one thing over another. Working 10 hours a work costs you 10 hours you could use to study, to join a club, to socialize with new friends, or even to catch up on needed sleep. Thinking this way demonstrates that working isn't free, i.e., you have to give to get.

---

58 https://www.nytimes.com/2015/07/04/your-money/its-summer-but-where-are-the-teenage-workers.html?_r=0

59 https://tcf.org/assets/downloads/sum_JAG_Paper_Nov_2013-1-2.pdf

Right about now it's probably clear that I'm not an advocate of working in your first semester with money as your goal, unless your money needs (like mine were) are truly real. The things you give up, as described in the previous paragraph, are far more than valuable than the moderate amount of money you'll accumulate.

One huge exception exists: becoming the dorm security check person. Why is this position different from others, you wonder? Simple. For the most part, this position allows you to study while you sit and check ID's every now and again. As long as you can discipline yourself to study in public, the opportunity cost of this particular job shrinks markedly. Moreover, this can be a way to meet your peers. Not the best way, mind you, but at least you're seeing and being seen. Two of the four costs of working, therefore, aren't as expensive, per se, with the dorm security job. Keep that one in mind.

2. To Meet People

Some students work to meet people. This goal makes more sense in many instances than the monetary one, though I maintain that the losses of study time and club interactions need to be factored into the decision-making process. The hardest thing about working any job this early in your college life is that at first, it's really hard to know how much time you need to study and to do your work. Until you get a sense of this, it's generally not wise to limit the amount of time you actually have.

Once again, exceptions occur. Meeting your fellow students, especially older students, is often easiest at work, and is certainly a worthwhile goal. If you are super organized and/or the kind of kid who actually does worse with any free time handed to you, then working, even this early in college, can be beneficial.

3. To Fulfill Work Study Requirements

This one is self-explanatory; if you're on work study, you have to work. What becomes important, then, is choosing the work you do based on your goals. If, for example, you are doing this solely because this is a way of defraying your college costs, then finding the easiest, most lucrative job available is best. However, if in addition to the money you are seeking engagement in your work, or looking to make friends, your choices will be different.

4. To Advance a Career Goal

Most students have no idea what career they might pursue when they first step foot on a college campus. Pretend you are different, and that you are dead-set on becoming a nurse, a doctor, a physician's assistant or some other medically-related position. Why would this field, more than say, business, merit early involvement? Blood, for example. It behooves a person interested in medicine to at least volunteer in a doctor's office or a hospital as soon as possible, just to be sure that they are not grossed out by the sight of blood, shots, tubes or patients in ill-fitting robes. The last thing you want to do is discover you are one of the "blood is yucky" crowd three years into a pre-med program.

This example is incredibly specific, and I'm struggling to think of others that would sway me into believing that working as a new college student in order to advance a career is a good use of your time. If you have such an example, meanwhile, more power to you.

Freshman Year, Second Semester

After a full semester, plus a winter break to re-charge, you'll have a much better sense of both how much time it takes you to properly study to achieve the grades you desire, along with how much time you need to socialize and to become immersed in your campus activities. This insight will guide you as to whether adding work to the mix is beneficial or, as alluded to above, still too costly to be worth it. In either case, always think back to your goals, as they help you analyze your plan accordingly. The last thing you want to do is take a low-paying, intense job if you are only working to help pay your bills. Likewise, working a boring desk job makes no sense, ever, even if your aim is to make friends with peers and older students.

Summer after Freshman Year

It saddens me when I hear of students killing themselves to get the perfect internship only a few months after they first embarked on the hugely transitionary journey that is college. Let's all settle down and understand what summer jobs at this point in a student's timeline are supposed to accomplish.

1. Keep Busy

    Your first summer job is extremely unlikely to be the key to your future success in that field. In fact, for the liberal arts students who are the primary readers of this book, I'll argue that getting a regular, seemingly crappy job is better than a fake internship with Uncle Bill, where you'll spend your summer scanning documents while asking yourself every moment why you made this terrible decision. Stay busy in the summer. Don't just sit around; work. And as all your friends will be doing the same thing, it's not as if you'll be missing out on anything anyway. What you learn from these so-called crappy jobs is vital to your ability to succeed in a "real" job in the future. (See below for a further discussion of this.)

2. Make/Save Some Money

    Work a summer gig that enables you to avoid working while you're at school (unless you want to do so).

3. Test a Passion?

    It's difficult to obtain a position of substance when you have no experience; testing a potential passion is therefore difficult to accomplish at this juncture. If you can do it, that's wonderful. If you can't, don't sweat it.

4. Learn to Solve Problems

    This needs to be the crux of every job you do. A good friend once explained to me that every business exists to solve problems. Problems are opportunities. Jobs you have at this age force customer interaction, which is real-time problem solving. Employees who stand out from their peers, the ones with a decided edge, are those who attain the ability to think independently and to develop solutions for problems, as opposed to becoming the type of employee who can only follow explicit orders.

Sadly, many hiring managers participating in a survey [60]contend that critical thinking and problem solving skills are lacking in college graduates.

The most frustrating thing about articles that tell you about what you're lacking is they rarely if ever tell you how to respond to your purported deficit. So how can you get better at solving problems and thinking objectively about situations? Put yourselves in as many tricky situations as possible. Immerse yourselves in your job, and try to change any aspect you think needs improving. Instead of floating, engage and seek change. As an ancillary benefit, I promise you'll actually enjoy yourself more too.

Two excellent examples of problem-solving summer jobs are painting houses and being a camp counselor.

Painting may be unglamorous, and even scary for an acrophobe like me, but College Works Painting Works is really onto something. Any college kids who haven't lined up anything for the summer, go to the site,[61] apply, and learn, Karate Kid-style.

Summer camp counseling, conversely, is the only thing more fun than being a summer camper. What could be better than being outside, at a place where you're loved and which is familiar, playing games with kids who adore you? When you come up with something, do it. Until then, don't look down on this job, which you really can do only once or twice.

This article [62]perfectly captures the summer camp versus more optically pleasing jobs debate.

Discussing his daughter's decision to be a camp counselor, the author avers, "Nor could I dispute her additional point that the work was incomparable preparation for the future, requiring the skills to manage group projects and

---

60 https://www.fastcompany.com/3059940/the-future-of-work/these-are-the-biggest-skills-that-new-graduates-lack

61 https://www.collegeworks.com/

62 https://mobile.nytimes.com/blogs/parenting/2012/05/29/the-camp-counselor-vs-the-intern/?_r=0&referrer=

motivate individuals, set goals and juggle tight schedules, and stay available for 24 hours a day, six days a week, in sickness and in health. .... But the clinching argument came from my daughter's impassioned defense of camp counselors, and her outrage that someone glancing at résumés would believe that a 20-year-old who fetches coffee at Google is more impressive than one who spends days and nights nurturing, teaching, organizing, comforting and inspiring. 'What I do there matters,' she insisted."

One commenter asserted, "I've had lots of jobs, and I talk about camp in every interview. I get every job because not only do I tell them how my camp experience has prepared me for the one I am currently applying for, but also because camp taught me to read people, to meet them and converse with them and impress them in a short period of time."

Another said, "As a former member of the 'real world' (lawyer for ten years turned summer camp director in New Hampshire), I can tell you unequivocally that the skills staff learn and utilize in the summer prepare them for the rigors of gainful employment life better than anything else imaginable. Is there a business owner or manager out there who wouldn't want to hire someone with creativity, grit, loyalty, compassion, the ability to solve problems and work as a team member, and seemingly endless and positive energy?"

I echo these themes. When I think of the best employees with whom I've had the great fortune of working over the years, it's always those people who learned something when they were young, whether at work, during school, at a club or wherever, and then transferred that quality to the job.

A super kid I'm thrilled to be mentoring, Jeffrey Horowitz, has worked as a camp counselor and in the summer of 2017 will be in charge of more than 100 kids, as well as of other counselors. Skeptics told him to "get a real job," when in fact he'll be doing more "real" work than almost anyone his age. Dealing with kids, being the boss of your peers, handling parental complaints – are as authentic as it gets. And trust me, a few years from now, Jeff will be able to transfer the stuff he learns here to any company, which in turn will be rewarded for hiring him.

Making copies at your dad's buddy's office might sound impressive, but it sucks, and no employer is fooled by it. Skip it, and do something real.

Sophomore Year, Winter Break and the Following Summer

By sophomore year, you'll have developed a much better sense of how to balance studying, socializing and working (if you choose to add a job to your schedule). At this point, you even may be able to focus on the loftier goals discussed above, such as advancing career paths and testing supposed passions. Regardless, you'll certainly be able to develop transferable qualities, while putting some money in your pocket.

For those of you who want or need to work during your sophomore (and junior) years, I ask: If there was no specific job that fit your major, what skills would you develop and how would you market those skills to get a job you wanted? Use the jobs you do during school to nurture specific skills you don't have now. Say you're studying psychology, human behavior, marketing or statistics, but a path as a psychologist, professor or statistician is unappealing. You discover that you enjoy applying your knowledge of human behavior to solve present day problems, and that you have an aptitude for statistics as well. A market research job, while not something you've considered or even something you necessarily could see yourself doing after graduation, would nonetheless foster the aforementioned abilities, abilities you can then use at your next position.

The National Association of Colleges and Employers (which goes by the cute pet name NACE) posits that jobs held during school offer students a chance to "apply their academic knowledge in work settings [63][and] are a vital component of a college education."

Some other specific skills to learn include the following:

1. Databases Like Excel and Access

    Oh the thrill of diving deep into an Excel spreadsheet, you say. Topped only by entering and manipulating data on Access. I can hardly type this through all the excitement. You may not want either of these databases to occupy significant amounts of your time post-college, but many of you may have to be at least proficient to succeed at your future position.

---

63 http://www.naceweb.org/advocacy/position-statements/united-states-internships.aspx

2. Sales

Sales, especially cold-calling, is easily the most dreaded task for most students (and most adults). Few people enjoy being constantly rejected. It's at best draining, and at worst completely demoralizing, to spend day after day getting hung up on by people to whom you're pitching a product. So why do it? There's nothing like repetitive rejection to help you develop a thick skin. The willingness to take and even seek constructive criticism, instead of seeking excuses, is what separates phenomenal employees from mediocre ones. Cold-calling may be the best means of achieving this.

Over the summer, a fabulous mentee of mine, Matt DiPasquale sold insurance, amongst the grimmest tasks I can imagine; he learned better sales techniques (a hard skill) as well as how not to internalize the negative feedback that is inherent with that type of job (a so-called soft skill). Unquestionably, Matt will be bringing this expertise to his next engagement.

3. Interview Practice

An overlooked but incredibly important benefit of interviewing for multiple positions is that you won't get them all. During this process, meanwhile, you'll start to recognize what you need to say to convey why you are an attractive candidate; this information cannot be gleaned from grabbing a job offered by your mom's cousin.

Some of your winter breaks can be long enough to allow you to get hired for seasonal work. You may earn enough, in fact, to allow you to focus on other things during the school year. Moreover, the skills you pick up in these jobs, which typically will have you dealing with the public, are invaluable.

Summer jobs are a bit of a different animal than the positions students encounter during the school year. Having spoken to scores of students, I've concluded that two factors contribute most to the success of the summer position:

1. The Job is Part of an Existing Program.

Too many students desperate for résumé-boosting material acquire summer posts through nepotism, i.e., someone giving you a job as a favor to your dad.

According to my family friend Eddie Sigman, who experienced both this type of summer job and one where, he was part of an existing program, the latter is far superior. In an existing program, you know what's expected of you; you have people there to guide and train you; you interact with other interns who can assist with questions you may have; and you potentially put yourself on a path for future permanent employment.

I'd add that the type of position Eddie describes affords you real responsibility and opportunities to learn important aspects of a job, a company, and an industry. Looking for typographical errors in an Excel document, or being given basically nothing to do for much of the day, gives you nothing. What's worse is that citing the latter job on a résumé can and likely will hurt you, for when a future employer asks in an interview what you did and what you learned, you're in trouble when your answers are "Not much" and "An eight hour day is really long when you have nothing to do."

Some people contend that despite the negatives I just described, any job will enable you to build your network. Surely some truth exists in that belief. That said, this is an incredibly inefficient means of meeting people, especially as the relationships you'll have had will have been shallow. And while some people make it their "job" to meet as many people as possible, this usually comes across as phony.

2. Interns Set and Reset Their Expectations

Talk to a summer intern and they'll frequently say they liked what they were doing, WHEN they had a chance to do real work. The problem is that many adults take vacations in summer, something parents can forget when junior is telling them that they've sat around for a week doing not much of anything because their boss is away.

So remember, students and parents: there will be times when there is simply less for you to do in the summer. Those times won't be fun. So make the most of the rest of your work experience, understand that this is pretty typical, and hope your boss remembers to bring you back some taffy.

You'll notice at this point that I haven't discussed the virtues of unpaid internships. Partially this is because the laws are changing when it comes to this, and partially this relates to my idea that you know your financial circumstances, and I don't. IF you can afford to work for free and IF the position fulfills your goals and IF the above conditions exist (i.e., this is a real job, not some "favor" someone is doing for you), then go for it, work for free.

Reading a recent NYT piece,[64] I was hugely impressed by this quote from Dominic Peacock, who was working as an unpaid intern at the National Congress of American Indians, "As long as I'm doing something that benefits the tribe, that's OK with me."

Combining selflessness (i.e., thinking of others) with crazy hard work is a powerful combination. Whoever hires this kid in the future will be fortunate.

Junior Year/Summer before Senior Year

Much of what was discussed above vis a vis sophomore year applies equally to junior year. Certain fields – consulting, accounting, and investment banking spring to mind – essentially require a junior year summer internship if one is to secure a position at that firm post-graduation. But these are the exceptions, and even within these fields it's possible to ultimately land a post without having gotten the plum summer internship at one of the huge firms that recruit on campus.

That said, this book is primarily focused on Liberal Arts students who are exploring various career paths (by that, I mean have little or no idea what they want to do after they leave the cozy college confines). If this describes you, it's worth reiterating that the primary objective you'll want to have for any work you take during junior year, or the summer following it, is to ascertain whether a particular career path appeals to you, or not (also hugely valuable).

Towards that end, I'd recommend a few tactics:

1.   Observe What Your Boss and Co-workers Do on a Day-to-Day Basis.

     If you notice, for example, that they are doing a lot of data entry type stuff, and you hate that kind of work, this might be a sign to consider other future options. Remember that what they are doing now, you'd be doing as a full timer. I am not

---

64 https://www.nytimes.com/2016/07/06/us/part-time-jobs-and-thrift-how-unpaid-interns-in-dc-get-by.html?_r=0

at all suggesting that you have to enjoy every minute and every aspect of your job; I am saying, however, that if your 25 year-old boss spends 75% of his day entering data into Excel, it's pretty likely that for three years that's your fate. If he spends 10% of his day on this grinding task, that's a completely different picture.

2.   Journal Journal Journal.

Write down everything that appeals to you about your jobs, both from a task perspective as well as from a cultural one. Were you part of a team or did you work alone? Did your boss give you feedback? How did your co-workers relate to one another? Were any of them hanging out together after work? How old was everyone there? Was the work you did in any impactful to the company? How? Were any suggestions you made for the company's website, or procedures, implemented? How did your co-workers react when you asked questions? The answers to these queries will be quite telling, and will help you identify patterns that subsequently indicate which fields are most suitable for you.

3.   Scrutiny over Money

It's not fair of me to second-guess anyone else's financial needs, so I won't. But assuming you're in a position where either the money you'll be earning is nice but not necessary for your survival, or where you are choosing between two positions that both pay well, remember your goal: discovering whether a job/field/company is right for you.

Consider the following scenario:

1.   Summer Internship A (SIA) pays significantly more (many thousands) than Summer Internship B (SIB).

2.   SIA is in NYC, near where you live, while SIB is in DC, where you've been once and don't know anyone.

Easy decision, right? A is clearly better. Except what hasn't been mentioned?

3.   SIB is in a field that greatly interests you, whereas SIA, eh, not so much.

4.   SIB stresses group networking and team-building, and you already like a number of the people in the program. SIA doesn't, and you don't like the people you know who are or were in the program.

Obviously, these are two amazing choices, and would qualify as a "problem" most students would kill to have. Still, the decision is difficult. So put on your noise-cancelling headphones and think: "What do I really want to get out of this internship?" If the answer is figuring out what you want to do after school, and interacting with people who might help you accomplish that goal, then the choice is clear, regardless of how many people tell you to follow the money.

4.   Be Brave

One of the most difficult choices students face is being offered a full-time job following a summer internship at a company they didn't like. It is so tempting to say yes; the security of having a full year where all one has to do is not fail out, knowing that in May, bang, a job awaits, can be incredibly alluring. Be brave, folks, and don't let your mouth say yes when your mind and heart are screaming no. A close friend told me the story about how he and a friend from college (who was a year older) obtained summer internships with a huge company. His friend accepted a job after graduation with that company and has felt stuck ever since. Obviously there's a lot more to it but while it's hard to say no, it's significantly harder to quit a full-time position and start over.

Senior Year
Hopefully by senior year of college, if you've taken the steps outlined in this book, you'll have uncovered a number of career paths that attract you. If so, senior year can be spent seeking internships/part-time positions where you enhance your skills while

making an impression on a future employer. Alternatively, or additionally, you can start the full-time job hunt (Chapter 15) in earnest.

If you're still searching for your true love, then by all means continue doing so. In that case, enter as many work situations as you can to test out what's right for you. If you can work multiple freelance gigs, do it. If you can't find appropriate "jobs," go volunteer.

Volunteering

Volunteering? Yuck. Whenever I say the word the reaction I get from college students is like asking an 8 year-old how he wants his broccoli cooked. Still, it's worth exploring here, for all the same reasons parents push their kids to eat vegetables.

Reasons Students Cite for Not Volunteering

Let's first set out the typical reasons kids put forth for why volunteering is not going to happen:

1. I Won't Like It.

   Really? How do you know this? Volunteering is really no different than any club you join, in that it puts you in touch with people who share your interests. Sure, maybe you'll find certain volunteer gigs are not for you. But writing off the whole process without trying a few things is like saying you hate Italian food because you don't like the Papa Johns' commercials.

2. I Don't Want to Be Bad at This.

   Fear of failure is best conquered when the stakes are lowest. The stakes cannot get lower than when someone is happy you've shown up.

3. That Sounds Like a Lot of Work.

   It might be; that's the whole point. Volunteering is often in lieu of work. It's designed to tell you whether you really like something, which is hard to do without any effort.

4. I'd Rather Hang with My Friends.

   Who wouldn't? You have two choices: either drag some of your friends along, or make new friends at the volunteer activity.

5. Who Does That?

   The old my friends don't do this so why would I canard. Here's one reason: because it works. I'd suggest that instead of thinking about volunteering as a stupid thing no one you hang with would do, you might be better off finding different people to hang with instead.

6. That Sounds Really Uncomfortable.

   OK, this one has some merit. By definition, it's hard to do things that make us uncomfortable. Here's the thing, though. Pushing past discomfort may be the one thing you end up being the most proud of yourself for doing in your four years of school. The student who goes to a hackathon and recognizes that while he has no technical abilities, he is able to get others to coalesce around and execute on an idea, will find that experience even more exhilarating than the person who's been coding apps for four years in high school.

Reasons to Volunteer

I've alluded above to a few of the many benefits of volunteering. Here's a few more:

1. Flexibility

   You can spend as little or as much of your time on a volunteer mission as you choose. You can quit if don't like it. You can't do this with a job. Advantage: volunteering.

2. Interest and Skill Development

   The principal reasons to engage in almost any activity are to hone in on your interests and to cultivate your skills. Volunteering is unique in its ability to help you meet both these targets. The freedom associated with volunteering allows you to throw yourself into it without fear of critique or failure. Sure, rules will exist, but when donating your time, generally your "bosses" will be mostly happy you are around at all.

3.   Experience

A volunteer pursuit is a LOT easier to achieve than finding a job or even an internship, yet it yields almost all of the same benefits as traditional work. You'll learn how to act on a job (to be discussed further, below), how to interact with peers and supervisors, how to manage your time, and how to relate to people of all different ages and types. Each of these experiences is critical to your future ability to be an asset at wherever profession you choose.

One last point I stress is to volunteer for yourself, not for your résumé. To ensure you think of volunteering in this light, I'd advocate not even putting this activity on your résumé. Use volunteering solely as a personal insight development tool. The purpose of volunteering is intensely personal. It's not meant for anyone else. It's to help you uncover who you are, what your interests are, and to gain experience performing various tasks to determine your level of interest in them, which is a huge, fundamental Catch-22. You need experience to get a job, but how do you get experience without the job? And how do you have any idea what job might be right for you without doing it?

Now if it turns out you love an activity, certainly it will make it onto your résumé. Remember, though: few things are more disqualifying than providing a list of volunteer activities in which you did basically nothing, then being asked about your time at a cancer walk by an interviewer who had cancer.

Where to Volunteer

Start your volunteer hunt by using the skills you know you have. If you've raised money for a charity in H.S., do it again in college. Gradually, add in other areas you'd like to try. Look for these opportunities in clubs, classes and dorms. You also can find great volunteer opportunities at volunteermatch.org,[65] idealist.org[66] (described further below), and LinkedIn's Volunteer Hub.[67]

---

65 https://www.volunteermatch.org/

66 http://www.idealist.org/

67 https://linkedinforgood.linkedin.com/programs/linkedin-members

Networking

As discussed at length in Chapter 10, networking is most effective when it's organic, i.e., when you have real relationships with people. With that in mind, do the following when seeking a job or an internship:

1. Think Hard About What You Enjoy.

    This could range from classes you've found stimulating to clubs you like to particular aspects of other jobs you've held. Write these things down.

2. Pattern Identification.

    Analyze and look for patterns in the items you noted in point one (you'll recall I mentioned this earlier in reference to job tasks – the idea is the same). Research how these patterns relate to specific companies, jobs, and fields of work, both through secondary sources (think online reviews) and primary sources (talking to people, or better yet, a mentor who has expertise in figuring these things out).

3. List of Names.

    Create a list of all the adults you know who have even the slightest connection to the fields you've identified in point two. All of them, including your parents' friends, your friends' parents, your relatives, your professors, your former bosses, etc. Remember our six degrees of separation philosophy: you never know who knows someone who can help you, until you ask.

4. Make Contact

    Send an email to everyone on your contact list. Explain what you're doing and what you're asking them for. Put out a specific time when you are available to talk, as people respond better to this than a general, "Do you have time?"

5. Converse.

> Not the sneaker brand. Talk. Ask people what they'd advise someone your age to do. Ask if they know people who can help you, or even who can hire you. Be interesting, and interested.

Some other networking ideas are as follows:

1. Keep Networking

> Networking doesn't end once you get a job. The aforementioned Jacob Heifetz-Licht (a fantastic Rutgers student who embodies the phrase "putting yourself out there") told me that networking is an activity that doesn't really stop. Jacob found that while working at a summer internship, he continued to meet people. His method was to connect with fellow Rutgers students also working in NYC and asking to let him shadow them for a few hours, or to meet for coffee or after work to chat about their job. What's the worst that can happen? Someone ignores you, or says no. Big deal.

2. Be Active

> When you are active in clubs and in class, meaning you participate, rather than attend, you'll simultaneously expand your current friend base (aka, your future network) while also making meaningful connections with adults. A huge benefit of this is meeting kids who are not like you, who are not in your classes or your dorm, and who you otherwise would never have met. Not only do you learn different perspectives, but you also open doors in unimaginable ways. By becoming a tour guide, for example, you develop a friendship with a fellow guide who is older and in the nursing program. You are studying business. Subsequently, you realize you're interested in helping a hospital with its new branding strategies; you turn to your friend, who's in the nursing program there now, and bingo, you have an in you didn't have before.

3. Ask for Recommendation Letters Immediately

Professors tell me that students routinely seek a recommendation years after taking a course taught by the professor. Compounding this error in timing, many students hadn't formed any type of relationship with the professor, who now is in the uncomfortable position of looking at past notes to glean any information about the student that might be informative. So at a minimum, seek a recommendation from a professor promptly upon the conclusion of a class, when you're fresh in that professor's mind.

Job Sites

I hesitate to even get into this given that technology changes so rapidly that by the time this book is out, three new work sites will have emerged. For now, these are some of the places I'd suggest students go to when seeking internships or jobs while in school (and frankly, after you graduate as well); the list is by no means exhaustive:

The Biggies

1. Indeed.com

    and

2. Ziprecruiter.com

Both Indeed and Ziprecruiter advertise tons of jobs and internships. The sites have easy-to-use features allowing you to narrow your search by geographical region as well as by keyword. The problem for job searchers is that everyone else is using these sites; feedback I've received from scores of students is that employers often don't respond to their applications. Still, these sites do have value and at a minimum will show you what's out there. Just don't think of them as the only or even the primary arrow in your quiver. One idea is to identify jobs in which you're interested, then use your networking abilities to help secure an interview. Not easy, but better than sending applications into the ether.

3. Craigslist.com

Yes, people, Craigslist is not just for buying bed-bug ridden furniture. In fact, Craigslist often has advertised positions the other sites don't, as it tends to cater to hyper-local, smaller employers. So include Craigslist in the mix.

4. Wayup.com

Wayup is an excellent site for people interested in the specific fields it covers. Unlike some of the other sites mentioned above, it is focusing on entry-level positions, so that's also a plus.

5. Your School's Job Board.

Never overlook the obvious. Many schools will have more postings from consultants, financial firms, investment banks and accountants, but even if these are not for you, some nuggets will present themselves too.

The Entry-Level/Internship Focused Sites

1. internships.com

As of September 2016, this site claims to have more than 178,000 internship listings across the country.

2. Looksharp.com

30,000+ is the number of internships this site professes to have, including paid, summer and non-profit.

The Industry-Specific Sites

1. Workinsports.com

    The name says it all; this site focuses on jobs in the sports world. From coaching to promotions, from management to sales and marketing, from technology to broadcasting, if you are looking to work in sports, this site has to be on your list.

2. Staffmeup.com

    This site advertises itself as listing "production jobs in film, TV, digital, media, and entertainment." Sounds exciting.

3. http://www.entertainmentcareers.net/jcat.asp?jcat=127

    Similar to the site cited above (you like what I did here, with the site cite thing?).

4. netimpact.org

    One of Net Impact's goals is to help students who are seeking to make changes in the world, whether that's in the environment, sustainability or similar arenas.

5. Idealist.org

    Similar to Net Impact, this entity is looking for people who want to "make a difference." If this sounds like you, this site may be hugely useful.

Other Sites

1. Google

    Here you thought you were going to get away without me mentioning the King of Search. The thing about Google is that if you're looking for basically anything, Googling is a good place to start. Job sites are no different.

2. LinkedIn

If you don't know what LinkedIn is, I'm afraid this book isn't all you'll need in your job search. For those of you thinking LinkedIn is merely a place to randomly "connect" with people you barely know, think again. Tons of companies (more big than small, generally) advertise jobs on this site. At a bare minimum, it should be a place you visit to see what they have and whether any of your connections (or their connections) can help point you in the right direction.

In Chapter 15, we'll go over some further LinkedIn techniques.

3. Handshake

Handshake, founded in 2014, seems to be trying to connect university recruiters, students and college career services. I'm not exactly sure what's different here, but this site bears monitoring.

How To Act At Work

I'll delve into the behaviors that make employers smile, and those that make them cringe, in a later chapter involving full-time work post-graduation. For now, let's simply remember a few rules:

1. Volunteer

Unlike what you may hear about volunteering while in the military (don't), volunteering as an intern is hugely beneficial. It doesn't matter if the tasks you're volunteering to do are "your job." In fact, it's even better if you're doing things in addition to what you were asked to do. Concentrate on areas you know a lot about. Dive into re-designing the company's website, if your boss gives you the nod. Improve the technology the company uses. Not technically oriented? Maybe you see that interns could learn from one another if they all ate lunch together; suggest this, and if approved, organize it.

Companies grow stale, and focus their efforts on today's problems. You are fresh, and don't have a stake in protecting your turf, or in making sure every fire is put out. Use that to your advantage.

2.   Open Up

The more you socialize with your fellow employees, in a positive way (no one likes a complainer, especially a young one), the more the group will feel like a community. Then the line between work and leisure fades a little. When you think of building a network, remember this.

3.   Learn More, Complain Less.

As long as your job is teaching you, you're fine. Even if what you're learning isn't exactly what you set out to discover. By all means, advocate for yourself, and ask to be put in positions to gain new skills. Just don't complain if sometimes what you are doing is repetitive, or seems beneath you.

4.   Be a Mensch, Not a Brat.

As an intern, you clearly have less responsibility than a full-time worker. Still, you owe your employer respect. Bailing out on a day of work because you have to go to the Hamptons may be tempting, but it's not cool. Treat an internship like you'd treat a job.

5.   Don't Be Like These Interns

Sometimes it's best to shut up [68]if you don't know all the facts. Anyone who has seen the clothes I wear knows I'm no fan of formal dress codes. But many companies feel differently. The quote I love in this story is that being an intern is akin to being a guest; you don't make the rules, you live by them. If there's something you object to, ask someone quietly and nicely why that rule exists. And if there's another person who seems to be flouting that rule, that's just none of your business. So don't ask.

---

68 https://www.yahoo.com/style/interns-get-fired-en-masse-after-protesting-dress-201632030.html

Conclusion

Getting any job is not a goal. Getting a job you want is.

Homework

1. Map out your plan for the next four years. It doesn't have to be novel length; use simple, brief bullets describing jobs you'd like to have each semester and during breaks. Adjust this list after each period has ended.

2. Go to Staples and buy a bunch of 49 cent notebooks. Bring them with you to class, to your job, to clubs, and to your volunteering activities. Write down whatever strikes you as important or interesting.

3. Ask your school's career center where you might volunteer, locally. They'll know.

4. With approval from your boss, organize an outing to a baseball game with all of your co-workers. It doesn't matter if you know a baseball bat from a fruit bat. You'll have multiple hours to really get to know your co-workers, any one of whom might be a vital future resource for you. (Credit for this suggestion is owed entirely to Gail Seiden, who tells me what I need to hear, not what I want to hear. When she gets done with her daily errands, that is.)

CHAPTER 13

Résumés and Cover Letters

Well, we've nearly reached the end. We've talked about classes, clubs and professors. We've discussed networks, mentors and internships. We cannot avoid the inevitable any longer: it's time to chat about résumés and cover letters.

I dread writing about this topic almost as much you dread reading it. So let's agree to get this over with, in as painless a way as possible.

Before I get into ideas I've gleaned about effective résumé writing, I'm compelled to point out the obvious: résumés DO NOT get you jobs. But bad résumés can cost you a job. The purpose of your résumé and cover letter is to earn an interview. That's it. These documents must tell an employer that you're both interested in working for them, specifically, and that you have the requisite skills to succeed at the job in question. Beyond that, what you say is superfluous.

Let's get to it, then.

Résumés

One Page Only Please

Until you're 24 or 25, you need to keep your résumé to one page. Even if you've saved a village in Africa, gotten As in 43 classes in a row, captained 6 teams and won an award for the most cheerful student in the debate club, you need to condense these accomplishments to one page.

If you have a ton of accomplishments from your time in college, then start cutting the material relating to your time in high school. If even that isn't enough, remove some of the bullets regarding each item; think two bullets per, rather than three to five. Absolutely delete things like hobbies or personal interests if including them pushes you onto a second page. Separately, play around with the format, using columns if a list is too long.

This article[69] touches on some other methods you can use to be part of the one page club.

Whatever You Write, Be Prepared to Discuss

I cannot stress this enough: the WORST thing you can do in your résumé is itemize a bunch of things in which your participation was effectively nil. As an interviewer, I eliminated people who, when asked what they did as Secretary of the Finance Club, responded, "Not much."

College students often worry about what activities will "look good on a résumé." But remember that a résumé only gets you an interview, not a job; in your interview, when a prospective employer asks you what you did in a club, internship, fellowship, job or class that you thought was significant enough to mention on your résumé, and your response is weak or evasive, you're in worse shape than had you not referenced this activity at all.

As I've noted throughout this book, the way to avoid the above scenario is to do the stuff in which you're interested. If you don't know what that is, try a bunch of things. Then go deep into the few activities that really capture your attention. That way, when an interviewer asks, you'll be able to answer, without faking it.

Another facet of this involves how you portray your various activities. One of my favorite mentees, the aforementioned Katie Gennusa, related that you should only bullet items you can support. In an effort to "beef up" an activity, you might be tempted to add to what you really did. If you can understand a little Spanish, but know that you'd be incredibly uncomfortable translating at a job, leave this off. If, however, you are fluent, absolutely add this detail. Resist the temptation to exaggerate, as an astute interviewer will think poorly of your character upon sussing out your B.S.

---

69 http://www.businessinsider.com/things-to-remove-from-resume-2016-11/#-6

Remember that the information contained on your résumé will have a significant effect on the questions you are asked in an interview. Make sure you know your résumé and prepare results-oriented stories to illustrate each of your accomplishments.

Different Job, Different Résumé

It sure is simpler to make one résumé and be done with it. Doing so is like answering every college essay question with the exact same essay – easy, but terribly ineffective.

Instead, adjust your résumé for different jobs. Obviously most of the information will remain the same; you'll create a template of sorts. Then, you'll want to change your wording to mimic the specific job listing to which you're applying. Different ads equal different résumés.

For example, if the job description uses a term like "fast-paced," review your history and find a position that accurately can be described as fast-paced — and then specify that precise term in a bullet under that entity. Sprinkle the terms cited in the ad wherever they fit; remember, I'm using the word sprinkle, and not deluge, for a reason. The idea is to demonstrate that you are an ideal candidate for a particular position, as opposed to a mere job-seeker. And even though your history may reflect that you are well-rounded, companies often are looking for specific skills. Stress that you have those; in your interview, you can explain how your other traits make you even more appealing.

In addition to job differences, certain fields require certain things. Consulting, for instance, is a very different animal. This book will not address all of the preparation you'll need to do if strategic, management consulting is your bag; still, check out this link [70] and this one [71] for some detailed tips.

Finally, though you'll be altering your résumé according to the position (and industry) in question, you must always be yourself. As discussed in the section above, you're not helping anyone by displaying attributes and accomplishments on a résumé that are either exaggerated or worse, don't reflect what you want to do and are skilled at doing.

---

70 http://consultingcareerconnection.org/index.php?option=com_content&view=article&id=68&Item id=36

71 https://managementconsulted.com/consulting-resumes/how-to-write-a-management-consulting-and-business-consulting-resume/

Specifics and Numbers

Statistics and numbers give weight and context to your résumé. Admittedly, as a college student, you may not have achieved sales results, saved an employer money or received a promotion. (Then again, maybe you did.) So think of these kinds of numbers as they relate to activities you have done. Rather than saying, "Ran marketing club and dramatically increased membership," state, "Headed membership drive for marketing club, increasing member roster from 25 to 45 students." If you were a tour guide, cite how many tours you led per semester. Worked behind the scenes for a theater or music production? Explain how many participants and attendees there were. Think of it this way: when you're tempted to use words like "dramatically" or "greatly," use a number instead.

Outcomes

Feedback and outcomes should rule your résumé. What happened, based on what you did?

I've seen this described effectively as the "result by action" structure. Here's an example: "*Increased dancer applications from 600 to 750 people by using consistent and targeted social media marketing initiatives.*"

Not every bullet point will yield to this structure. Somewhere between none and all is what you're targeting.

Action Verbs

Harvard put out a lengthy "how to" on writing résumés which is especially instructive when it comes to verb choice. Besides the incredible list of action verbs, the Harvard guide has other tips you may want to peruse.

White Space is Your Friend

The instinct to cram in as much data as possible into your résumé is understandable, especially because you only have a page with which to work. But a résumé is not a cheat sheet your professor allows you to bring in for an exam. The person reading your résumé likely won't even give it more than a glance if the text is so dense as to produce an immediate headache.

The cure for an overly packed résumé? White space. White space is the space that is, well, white (meaning empty). White space helps direct the reader's eye and focuses attention where you want them to look.

White space emerges both from simply using less text, as noted above, as well as from your design techniques. Use bullets, line breaks and shorter sentences. Generally, this should be enough to ensure an appealing visual effect. If you need to do more, play around with the design. I've seen an excellent résumé that used columns instead of the traditional straight chronology approach. That said, be aware of being too fancy. The résumé's job is to get you in the door for an interview. It's not part of your art portfolio.

One other cautionary note comes from Amanda Augustine of TopResume, who said in a *Business Insider* story [72] that having too many bullet points is "death by bullets."

According to Augustine, "if absolutely everything is bulleted, it has the same effect as big dense blocks of text — your eyes just glaze over it." Use bullets only to draw attention to the most important information. "If you bullet everything, *everything* is important, which means really nothing stands out."

Minefields

<u>Lying</u>

I've seen surveys indicating that about half of job applicants lie on their résumés. My former company examined résumés as one part of a detailed investigation into people's careers. I'm not sure whether the 50% figure cited in surveys is accurate, but I can say with certainty the number isn't zero.

The problems with lying on a résumé are twofold. First, getting caught exaggerating your results creates a negative perception that's hard to overcome. Second, lying today is permanent, thanks to digital technology. When I handed my résumé to a prospective employer in 1987, that résumé ultimately was discarded. Today, résumés typically are emailed, or uploaded, creating a record of sorts. Additionally, while you can adjust your LinkedIn

---

72 http://www.businessinsider.com/biggest-mistakes-people-make-their-resume-expert-topresume-amanda-augustine-2016-1

profile, nothing prevents someone from taking a screen shot for later comparison.

Don't lie. Take your chances that who you are is who they want. If you want to be a better candidate, be that by actually achieving things, rather than saying you did.

Grammatical/Spelling Errors

Saying you pay attention to detail and misspelling attention on your résumé is the kind of mistake that gets you in an article on dumb résumé mistakes. It won't get you a job, however.

Use spell check. Then go back and re-read your résumé, slowly, looking for missing words, missing punctuation marks and spelling errors spell check might miss. After that, have someone else do another review, just in case you've become blinded to your own mistakes. Take this seriously, as nothing spells "next" faster than typos.

Being, um, Stupid

A CareerBuilder survey, which included more than 2,100 full-time, U.S. hiring and human resources managers, revealed some incredible errors job candidates make.[73]

- An applicant named Fred's last name was auto-corrected from "Flin" to "Flintstone." I'd actually consider hiring this person just because this is so bizarre. But that's me.

- An applicant listed a skill as "taking long walks." Something he undoubtedly has a lot of time for, given he won't have a job.

- An applicant claimed he would work harder if paid more. Even if true, keep this little self-analysis to yourself.

---

73 http://www.prnewswire.com/news-releases/careerbuilders-annual-survey-reveals-the-most-outrageous-resume-mistakes-employers-have-found-300331933.html

- An applicant wrote the following at the end of their résumé: "I didn't really fill this out; someone did it for me." No comment necessary.

Minor Details Matter

<u>No More Home Address</u>

This isn't an issue the way spelling errors are. In the age of data security, however, adding your home address to your résumé can create a problem, and offers no real upside. Lose it, and stick with an email address.

<u>Font</u>

Once again, choosing Times New Roman as your default font isn't a death knell. But some experts[74] believe that similarly professional fonts like Helvetica, Garamond, and Proxima allow your résumé to stand out while remaining polished.

<u>URL of LinkedIn</u>

Your LinkedIn profile may have some information you want to share that you cannot fit on your résumé. Include the URL to your profile on your résumé and voila, problem solved.

<u>Professional Email Address</u>

No more ashleyrulz99@gmail.com. Bye bye hotchick@yahoo.com. Create an email address that's simple and professional. Your name plus gmail will do.

<u>Name Your File Correctly</u>

Thomas Williams.Résumé is fine. "My résumé," "new résumé" or "résumé 2016" will get lost in the deluge of documents an employer receives. Use some combination of your name and the word résumé, and that's it.

---

74 https://mic.com/articles/116920/writing-a-resume-here-s-the-most-popular-font-you-should-never-use#.FxJgNBw7O

Track Changes

Don't let these be visible.

Consistency

Staying consistent may seem picayune but like the items above, not doing so can be costly. If you use two spaces after a period, do so throughout your résumé. Mind your margins (I feel like a fourth grade teacher here). Keep your spacing even. All of this creates a positive impression on the reader.

Getting Past the Machines

The online application process certainly has made it easier for you to seek multiple jobs with minimal effort. The downside of applying for jobs online is that employers, especially larger companies, may use an applicant tracking system (ATS). In Chapter 15, I'll outline all the ways you can use to get around the mechanical résumé screeners; for now, let's focus on what to do if you have no choice but to go through the ATS filter.

Some of the advice [75] given by industry experts [76] includes items we've talked about earlier, from eliminating grammatical/spelling errors to using industry and job-specific keywords on your résumé. Other tips are more sophisticated, like mimicking Google search engine optimization (SEO) techniques. This article [77] in *IT World* suggests that, "the 'hack' to finding the way through the filter is use the job application to see what their imputed query would have been based on the language they use in their job application, and trying the best to match it." The article quotes Larissa Cox, described as a marketing manager who is adept at SEO and social media marketing, citing the following SEO techniques as being applicable to résumé writing:

- "Using multiple 'related' words throughout the résumé, [e.g.] 'Photoshop, Creative Cloud, graphic design, designing.'"

---

75 http://www.businessnewsdaily.com/9358-digital-job-search-guide.html

76 https://www.amazon.com/Resume-Bible-Only-Writing-Youll-ebook/dp/B00QR82SK4/ref=sr_1_1?tag=itworld030-20&s=books&ie=UTF8&qid=1418375230&sr=1-1&keywords=resume+bible

77 http://www.itworld.com/article/2877257/get-your-resume-past-the-robots-how-to-beat-hrs-mechanical-gatekeepers.html

- "Keyword density of specific words matching emphasized skills in the job posting."

- "Keyword matching. Do they use the word 'online' instead of 'digital,' 'internet,' or 'web?' I change my vernacular to match."

- "Specific reference to software or other tools, especially if they have mentioned specific programs in their postings. Instead of vague terms like 'social media management,' I use specific programs like 'Hootsuite,' 'Buffer,' or 'SproutSocial.'"

Creativity

For certain jobs, being creative with your presentation can help you stand out. I'm not sure sending your résumé in a box of donuts [78] will get you an interview with an accounting firm. But the same approach might get you a better reception from a digital marketing firm, an advertising agency or a PR firm. Know your audience.

Examples

Feel free to contact me for examples of effective résumés.

Cover Letters

Many of the guidelines set forth for writing your résumé are equally valid when it comes to putting together cover letters. Spell checking, ensuring your grammar is spot on, using keywords related to the particular job and industry, and mimicking language used in the job advertisement are all effective and necessary.

The key to a cover letter is demonstrating to the employer that you really want that job, not just any job. This requires two things:

1. Research. Find out about the company and the position both from the ad itself as well as from other sources like the company's website, news stories and social media postings.

---

78 http://www.cnbc.com/2016/10/13/6-of-the-most-creative-resumes-weve-ever-seen.html

2. Truthfulness. Do not apply for jobs you don't want. You're wasting your time and the time of the interviewer. It's one thing to interview as "practice" for a job you think you might want, only to discover it's not for you. It's quite another to interview when you are certain you'd never take the job in question.

Here again, reach out to me for samples of effective cover letters.

Homework

1. Ask your parents and friends to review your résumé and then remind you of activities or skills you may have inadvertently omitted. Add these.

2. Similarly, have friends and parents gently grill you on your bulleted items. Delete the ones that sound phony.

3. Beg your English major buddy to peruse your documents for spelling and grammatical errors.

CHAPTER 14

Interviews

We're coming to a close, people, and now we're getting into some of the really granular stuff. Strap in.

When I think about how to describe the interview process, I harken back to the over 1,000 interviews my team and I conducted during the last two decades. These memories, some old and many quite fresh, demonstrate that the methods of successful job interviewing haven't really changed; what's more, these techniques are relatively easy to learn, with practice.

So as my grammar school principal Ernie Finizio (with whom I had more than a passing acquaintance, unfortunately) used to say, "Without further ado:"

Purpose

The purpose of an interview is for you to express what you've done, what skills you've developed in the process, the proof of those skills, and why those skills and interests make you a viable match for the particular job in question. Ultimately, you need to convince the company that you are good for and really want the job they have, as opposed to being a person who's merely seeking any job. As I used to say at the onset of every interview, the interviewer can be fooled into thinking you're into whatever he's offering. Sadly, this helps neither party, for if three months after getting hired you confirm your belief that you didn't want the job, you will either be ready to quit or find yourself terminated, as most people cannot do well at something they hate.

Don't try to pass the lie detector test here. Your "job" is to understand whether this job is right for you, as much as it is for the company to determine whether you are a good fit for them. Below we'll go over how.

Story-telling

Step one in any good interview is to understand that essentially an interview is nothing more than a conversation. Although you might be nervous and the interviewer might be tired, bored, or distracted, the more of a personal connection you can make, the more memorable you'll be.

But how do you form a connection, you might ask. Simple: with stories. Let me assure you that no interviewer will remember the person who goes on and on describing himself as hard-working, a team player and someone who learns quickly. Sure, these are all wonderful traits, and they're certainly better than being lazy, selfish and dumb. But traits are only memorable if they are attached to anecdotes. Asked to describe yourself, most people start out by listing their best qualities, as if reading a recipe out loud. One teaspoon of hard-working. Snooze. Add one cup of quick learner. Boooooring. Stir in a tablespoon of team playing and you're in full scale Ambien mode. Instead, use a story that illustrates your skills. Interviewing for a social media marketing post, and asked to describe yourself, you reply, "I love to influence the way people buy through social media. This past summer, I was fortunate enough to have an opportunity to work for AAA Marketing, and on one campaign, we were trying to help a local tutoring company expand to nearby towns. We first spoke with some of their existing customers, and then we analyzed the nearby competition. We ended up determining that posting an ad on a parents group in Facebook would be the best way to reach the right people, and the company got 15 new clients from it. I realized that this is what I want to be doing a lot more of and therefore I'm excited about the chance to work for your firm." An interviewer almost certainly will follow up with questions, because you've told an engaging story; this, my friends, will result in you being remembered.

Think of stories demonstrating how you've solved problems in lieu of just following orders. Stories that prove how passionate you are about a particular issue. Stories that show your demeanor, especially when faced with others who are unpleasant or even rude.

My number one tip for future interview success is thus this (say that five times fast): **keep a journal during all four years of school**. I know, I know, a journal sounds lame. Nerdy. Whatever. Just f...in do it anyway. I'm not suggesting it needs to be something fancy. It doesn't need to be shown to anyone else, ever. It's really just taking notes, like for class, except instead of throwing it away at the end of a semester, you'll keep adding to it. Unless your parents were elephants or you have an eidetic memory, like Dr. Sheldon Cooper of The Big Bang Theory, you will absolutely forget most of the little events that mark you as unique. Gather your stories, one day at a time. Four years later, you'll be really thankful you did. (P.S. A special thanks here to Erin Weaver, who's responsible for this notion.)

Once you commit to writing down tidbits that speak to what you find stimulating as well as what events intimately describe your interests and skills, you're ready. Gather your stories from day-to-day events (think classes, group projects, club meetings), or from longer term commitments like summer jobs and internships. Ask any recent graduate if they wished on an interview that they were more prepared to answer a question posed with an anecdote. Avoid that feeling of dread by taking note of whatever you find interesting, funny, or illuminating.

Unfortunately, students often don't recognize when they have done something an interviewer will find significant. A kid with whom I'm working transferred into his university's honors college his sophomore year. He advised me that he really had to push himself to catch up to the other honors students, all of whom he thought seemed to be at a level higher than he was. He described this as using their drive to fuel his own. I immediately told him that this would be a great story to tell in a future interview; he seemed baffled by this, so I explained my reasoning: this story exemplifies how instead of being envious and creating excuses for himself, he did the opposite, ultimately resulting in him being every bit as successful as his peers. You think an employer could use a guy like this?

OK, so it's senior year, you're armed with multiple tales you've jotted down during the past four years, and you're about to embark on the interview process. What now? Like any good politician, you'll practice answering a variety of seemingly different questions using the five to six stories that best illustrate who you are, why you're unique, and what makes you someone who can do the job in question. Practice is the operative word here; it takes some time reviewing your answers, both in terms of content and presentation, for you to sound your best. As much as you might be tempted to wing it, don't. Preparation and practice will yield significantly better results; interviewing without either is like taking a part in a play, never reviewing your lines, and then hoping on opening night you miraculously avoid seeming like a buffoon. More on preparation mode is below.

As stated earlier, I am not a fan of the so-called "practice" interview, i.e., going on interviews for jobs you definitely would never take. This isn't practice; it's a waste of everyone's time. When companies ask why you want to be there, and the truth is you don't, making something up is not helping them, clearly, and isn't helping you either. Instead, if you want to "practice," identify companies with jobs that sound at least moderately appealing. On the interview, you can determine if you truly want the position, and the interview will be useful one way or the other (you'll either want the job, which is great, or you won't, which is also excellent insight and will allow you to hone your future search based on the information you gained).

Preparation

Below are some frequently asked interview questions, followed by typical reactions (in bold) students think to themselves the first time they hear these questions:

1. Tell me a little about yourself. **Yikes, really? Where do I begin?**
2. Who is the worst (best) boss/subordinate/classmate you have ever worked with? **I thought I wasn't supposed to be negative in an interview?**
3. What kinds of people do you find it difficult to work with? **Same as above.**
4. Describe a situation where your judgment proved to be valuable. **My judgment? When would I have exercised judgment?**
5. Do you work better under pressure or with time to plan and organize? **Uh oh, which answer do they want to hear?**
6. What is more important– completing a job on time or doing it right? **Same as above, plus this interview sucks.**
7. What are your strengths and weaknesses? **My strengths I can list, but what should I say about weaknesses?**
8. What are you most proud of? **Does graduating with a 3.3 count?**
9. What kinds of decisions are most difficult for you? **The ones like this, where I don't know what to say.**
10. How would your boss/friends/co-workers, etc. describe you? **They'd say I'm loyal and funny, but does that matter?**
11. What three words would you choose to best describe yourself? **See above.**
12. Why do you consider this to be a good opportunity? **Because I really need a job.**
13. Describe how you allocate your time and set your priorities on a typical day. **Am I supposed to mention the time I spend at the gym and on Xbox?**
14. Are you a better planner or implementer? **Great – another trick question.**
15. Why are you interested in this internship/job? **As I said before, because I need a job to get out of my parents' house.**

16. Why should we consider you? **I'm hard-working and a quick learner, but ugh that sounds so generic.**

17. Why are you interested in this industry/company? **You do really cool stuff. And my dad told me to apply here.**

18. Tell us about your knowledge of this company. **I found some stuff online but I'm not sure it's enough.**

19. Give an example of how you dealt with a conflict with another person/customer/classmate/professor, etc. **If I answer honestly, won't I look bad?**

20. Tell me a story either personal or professional that paints a picture of you. **Damn – I knew I should have prepared more.**

Sound familiar? Probably. Sound good? No. Sound hopeless? Definitely not. So let's address how we can turn these thoughts around.

As alluded to above, interviewing is a bit like acting. For most people, interviewing can be stressful; you feel like you're performing, but without a script. But even if you'd never perform on a stage or in front of a camera, all of you graduates and soon-to-be graduates can and must "perform" in front of an interviewer.

Asked what makes a great actor, Laurence Olivier (old folks' version of, say, Robert Downey, Jr.), responded, "The humility to prepare and the confidence to pull it off." Preparation will always trump nerves.

Preparing for interviews is like preparing to drink tequila (which of course none of you under-age people are doing); three steps make the process, and skipping any one of them makes the whole thing less effective.

1. *The salt*: research the company, the position you are seeking and even the interviewer before you show up. Nothing is worse from an interviewer's perspective than a candidate who is uninformed. This is a death knell for you, and frankly, it should be. If you cannot be trusted to at least find out what my company does and what the current position is about, how can you be trusted to handle a work assignment once you get here?

   Today, researching a company is remarkably simple. Between Google and social media, you should be able to determine more than enough details to discuss. Look for questions you can ask; this is made easier, naturally, if you legitimately have things you want to know. As a starting point, always ask, in a way that makes you feel comfortable, what a typical day is for a new hire in the role for which you're interviewing. Other good ones include, "What are the characteristics of those who succeed at this company?" and "What is the best/worst part of your day?" Have the interviewer explain how much independence you'll have, how you'll be supervised, and overall, what a new hire is expected to know and do on their own.

The answers will tell you a number of things, including whether this is a job that truly appeals to you. Furthermore, additional questions will emerge organically based on the response to this question, as well as to others you ask during the interview. Finally, you'll add in specific questions you derived from your online research.

2. *The tequila*: review and practice your stories, fitting them into the questions a company is likely to ask you. We'll go over a list of some standard interview questions momentarily. Meanwhile, recognize that companies will ask specific questions based on the nature of the company and especially, the nature of that job. For a sales position, an interviewer will ask how you handle rejection. A TV production job is one in which you'll almost always be working as a team, so expect questions about how you handled group projects. Any job that involves a lot of writing will lead an interviewer to question the thickness of your skin, i.e. how you handle criticism. Anticipate these questions, and be ready with the stories that depict how you've handled previously yourself in these scenarios.

3. *The lime*: review standard interview questions, like those cited above, and have your answers, and stories, ready. The good news is that you can fit each story to multiple questions. Your answer to how you'd describe yourself, for example, can be based on the same anecdote you'll tell for the question how would others describe you. The same goes for responding to why you think the job is a good opportunity for you, why you are interested in that job, why you are interested in that company and why you are interested in that industry. If you think about the above questions, you'll see, in fact, that they can be grouped as follows:

Group 1: Who are You?

Tell me a little about yourself.

What are your strengths and weaknesses?

How would your boss/friends/co-workers, etc. describe you?

What three words would you choose to best describe yourself?

Describe how you allocate your time and set your priorities on a typical day.

What are you most proud of?

Tell me a story either personal or professional that paints a picture of you.

Group 2: The negatives

Who is the worst (best) boss/subordinate/classmate you have ever worked with?

What kinds of people do you find it difficult to work with?

What kinds of decisions are most difficult for you?

Group 3: Why us?

Why are you interested in this internship/job?

Why do you consider this to be a good opportunity?

Why are you interested in this industry/company?

Tell us about your knowledge of this company.

Give an example of how you dealt with a conflict with another person/customer/classmate/professor, etc.

Group 4: Why you?

Describe a situation where your judgment proved to be valuable.

Why should we consider you?

Group 5: The tricks

Are you a better planner or implementer?

Do you work better under pressure or with time to plan and organize?

What is more important – completing a job on time or doing it right?

Using five stories, told from slightly different perspectives and/or using more or less (or different) details, you can cover 20 questions in an engaging and effective manner. You must have answers to these and similar questions in advance; winging it won't work.

End of an interview

The end of an interview is always a bit odd. Even when the conversation seemed to have gone swimmingly, it can be unclear what's next.

Here are two recommendations:

1. Ask, specifically, "What's the next step? Do you need anything else from me?"

These questions are designed to ascertain whether the company will be asking you in for another interview, and if so, when. Either way, it's a lot better than simply waiting around not knowing anything.

2. Make sure you have the interviewer's contact details. Ask for a card. Or just write it down. Then get ready to send your thank you email (below).

Follow ups/Thank yous

Everyone knows about the follow-up email, but many people stress the details. Do I email from the parking lot? Wait for two days so as not to appear too eager? Send a fruit basket from Edible Arrangements? No – weird; no – this isn't a dating game; and no, definitely not.

When you get home from an interview, depending on your travel situation, is usually the perfect time for the thank you follow-up email. You'll want to be succinct, but you'll also want to emphasize the following items:

1. Your passion for this particular job and company, which you'll name.
2. That you readily accept constructive criticism and are always looking to improve.
3. You are confident you will be a valuable employee.

The key is to make these points using specific details about the job gleaned from your conversation, as well as via stories you told in the interview (or even those you didn't). "I'm really excited for the opportunity to be an account executive at XYZ Advertising. Your campaigns for everything ranging from Miller Lite beer to Acura have stuck with me since I was young, and I'd love the chance to liaise between the creative people and your clients. As I mentioned, I had a chance to work with ABC Agency this summer, and my time there cemented my interest in this field as well as my belief that I can be a valuable contributor to your firm. You explained that the account executive position comes with a fair amount of tension, given that the clients will sometimes expect things that the creative team cannot deliver, or will change their minds seemingly capriciously. I recognize the stakes are much higher, but my many waiter jobs (highlighted on my résumé) have taught me the diplomacy necessary to manage situations where neither the customer nor staff is satisfied. I look forward to utilizing this skill for XYZ. Thank you again for your consideration."

Informational interview

What is an informational interview, anyway? At the risk of insulting Dr. Martin Luther King here, an informational interview is the time for you to declare that you have a dream. Whatever it is that you truly would like to do, however far-fetched it might seem to be, has to be discussed for the informational interviewer to provide you with, well, information. You simply cannot get what you might want without explaining what it is. Certainly this must be done in the right way; still, it's better for you to stumble a bit with your presentation than to pussyfoot around and get nothing valuable in return.

Most people insist that an informational interview is something where you ask the other person about "their path." This is fantastic, if that person is a few years older than you. But as most of you are doing these types of calls with your parents' friends or associates, asking about how they got to the executive position they have now is hardly relevant to you. Nor is discovering how they started 30+ years ago. Tell this person what you hope to accomplish, tempered by understanding that this is a long-term goal and not something you expect to happen immediately. Then ask how can you achieve that goal AND whether there are paths/jobs/companies that you could take that you may not even have considered.

Another benefit of the informational interview is gathering details about a job/industry/company that seems appealing, but about which you know very little. Think of this exercise as job shadowing, but on the phone. Here again, asking about specific day to day job tasks will clue you in as to whether this position resonates with you. Just be very clear that you don't use this as a phony way of getting a job; interviewers see through this, and get really irritated that you've misled them.

More on informational interviews can be found here.[79]

---

79 http://www.youthcareercompass.com/wp-content/uploads/2016/07/Informational-Interview-Guide_Youth-Career-Compass.pdf

Further interview tips (courtesy of my fine former co-workers at BackTrack)

1. Ask about the dress code before you arrive.

2. Prepare for "trick" questions by developing your spin on your life events. Work with someone to develop this "spin." "I worked at a dress shop" isn't nearly as effective as, "I went to NYC, selected merchandise, then decorated the store window and ascertained what sold, and what didn't."

3. Know who you're scheduled to meet with when you arrive.

4. Show up on time, and not more than 10 minutes early. If your interview is at 2PM, don't laugh and say you just got up (true story – this happened).

5. Have a good handshake – nothing moist, lingering, bone-crushing or dead fish like.

6. Hygiene.   Enough said.

7. Ask spontaneous questions. Generate questions that result from the actual interview that is taking place. This shows you're listening and thinking. Be conversational and you'll be fine.

8. Ask questions, period. When companies interview someone they always ask, 'What are your questions?' When an interviewee says none, you're pretty much done. If you've exhausted a few questions but are still willing to struggle, to *dialogue*, even it is to draw the interviewer's attention to the question s/he has already asked, the company will be more impressed. Make sure these relate to what you'll be doing, and not things like "What's your vacation policy?" or "How much do I get paid?" (Save for this when an offer is made.)

9. Treat the interviewer as a resource. You are interviewing the employer, not just the other way around. The interviewer's life won't change too much as a result of this conversation, but yours might.

10. Maintain eye contact – but don't be creepy about it.

11. Be conscious of your tone and speed. Mirror the other person's movements; don't cross your arms or look at your feet (your shoes are great, but no one cares.)

12. It's OK to admit your weaknesses to the interviewer. Example: "I'm so excited to work here that I know I'm talking too fast. I'll slow down." This can actually be endearing.

13. It's fine to be lighthearted, but be wary of making too many jokes. Be thoughtful.

14. Be able to discuss your past in a way that is not difficult or annoying or terribly boring. What have you liked in college so far, or in other jobs you've had?

15. Be eager but not desperate. It shouldn't seem like the end of the world, because it isn't. Explain your passions – what gets you juiced?

16. Take your time to answer. Breathe.

17. Come prepared with writing or portfolio samples, as applicable. Also, bring a short list of references, including emails and phone numbers – even if your résumé says "references available upon request." Assume that the interviewer is going to like you enough to want them.

18. Be transparent about upcoming vacations/weddings/etc. before accepting an offer.

Whatever you do, DO NOT DO THE FOLLOWING:

Go to an interview with your mom, and ask that she be present during the interview.

Asked what want to do in your life, don't giggle and say, "I don't know."

Be a victim, i.e., don't present yourself as someone who's been wronged at previous jobs. Employers hear that and are immediately nervous and off-put.

Asked where you want to be in five years, don't answer with something that is completely different than the job for which you are interviewing, unless it's on the career path of that position.

Homework:

Checklist in preparation for your interview:

1. Have you researched the company and the job? Write what you've learned, everything from dress code, to where they are, to what they do.

2. Write three specific and general questions to ask.

3. Briefly highlight your five top interview stories.

4. Label the interview questions grouped above with the interview stories that apply to each category.

5. Practice your answers, out loud, with a grown-up familiar with interviewing. Adjust statements, body language and tone according to specific feedback. Practice again.

6. During the interview, take notes (using a pad, not your phone). When the interviewer mentions something you want to discuss further, jot it down.

CHAPTER 15

Jobs After College – The Holy Grail

Here we are. Leaving college. Getting a job. Becoming an adult (ugh). The source of your senior stress. The "oh crap what do I know now" moment. Hopefully, by implementing the tactics set forth in this book, you're prepared for what comes next. Maybe you're even excited about it.

In this chapter, we'll talk about your first job versus your "career." We'll figure out how to figure out what jobs are right for you. We'll discuss how to get a job, how to accept or reject an offer, and how to interact with your colleagues and your bosses. Away we go.

Overall Things To Know

You're Looking Only for Your First Job. It Won't Be Your Last

In the 1950's, people landed a job with a company and often then remained at that company for their entire career. Now? Even if you love a particular company, a specific field and even one job within that field and company, there's no guaranty the company or even industry will even be around for the next decade, much less the next 40 years. Tech companies come and go as they get obliterated by the next hot thing. The news media faces an uncertain future. Energy companies will undoubtedly shift radically as climate change proliferates.

None of this is designed to scare you. In fact, it's the reverse. Understanding that your first job is just that, your first job, empowers you to take some risks. If you've studied marketing, and think you might like digital marketing, you can test this hypothesis with either a marketing company specializing in this area, or with a company that is looking to hire an internal person to help with its web presence.

Once there, you'll get a much better sense of what aspects of the job you like, and which you don't. If you discover that what really gets you excited is designing websites, go ahead and learn programs like InDesign and Photoshop (among others). You can take these skills to a similar firm, or a completely different one, like an advertising agency. While it's important to commit yourself to your first job, keeping in mind that it won't be your last reduces the stress of thinking this job has to be "perfect."

Aziz Ansari's book on dating astonishingly touched on something relevant to job hunting. Ansari quotes Barry Schwartz and Sheena Iyengar (both authors, psychologists and professors), who describe what they call a "paradox of choice."[80] "Maximizers" are people who weigh every option; they often get "better" jobs but are less satisfied with them, according to Schwartz and his colleague Andrew Ward. Satisficers, conversely, make decisions more quickly, but become quite content with their "lesser" jobs. The current term for a maximizer, to me, is FOMO (the fear of missing out) which I've touched on earlier in this book. When you're looking for a job, don't create a fantasy job that meets every one of your desires perfectly. Find a job that seems to meet your top two to three things, and go from there.

You'll Always Find Something When You Look

Simply preparing for the interview process yields tangible benefits. My son Jackson was seeking a summer internship with a consulting company. This required him to review multiple case studies, as the interviewers asked in-depth questions about real-life consulting scenarios. Jackson described this practice as having "unlocked" critical thinking skills he hadn't previously exhibited; he now sees practical applications for these skills in many parts of his life. Even if you don't get the job you were seeking, it's always useful to learn a new skill, especially one that's transferable. Remember, too, that once you're finished with your preparation, it's not as if you now turn this skill off. It's yours to utilize.

I Don't Want to Be an Adult Yet

Unfortunately, you can't be a Toys R Us kid [81] forever. But I get it. You're about to graduate and you're leaving seemingly the best time of your life for ... uncertainty? Many of you may have few definitive job prospects. You have to figure out where to

---

80 https://www.swarthmore.edu/SocSci/bschwar1/Choice%20Chapter.Revised.pdf
81 http://lessthanjake.wikia.com/wiki/I_Don't_Wanna_Grow_Up,_I'm_a_Toys_R_Us_Kid

live, navigate a new social life, and make money. Everything changes at once, and a little harshly. Tackling all of the above issues at once is overwhelming.

Here's the thing, though: you're not yet an adult. You're still living at home. Most of you are not married. You don't have kids. So take it easy. Getting a job is just one step in your process.

Have you ever watched a baby learn to walk? A baby doesn't go from lying on its back crapping it's diaper one day to popping up and walking the next. First it learns to sit up. Then it crawls (often backwards at first), then does the crab walk. After this, it gets up by holding onto the couch, then takes a few halting steps and falls, and then, finally, it walks.

Except for the diaper part, this is what you'll do. Let your focus be entirely on securing a job. Don't worry about everything else, which will take care of itself once you have a job. Money? You'll have some with a job (maybe not as much as you want, but enough to live on). New friends? These emerge once you move and begin to socialize in new areas. Moving out of your parents' house? Totally possible once you have a job and roommates, depending on where you choose to live. The key is not to worry about all of these things at once.

Getting a Job Is a Job

Be prepared to work. Hard. Your job hunt is a full-time endeavor. Understanding this doesn't make the search fun, but it does make it bearable. The payoff is that actually working is far more rewarding, in so many ways, than looking for work. Let that be your motivator when you get annoyed, discouraged or agitated.

You're Not Alone

As mentioned previously, millennials mostly don't admit their fears and vulnerabilities to other millennials. We talked about the Facebook Fishbowl effect, the phenomenon of skewed results where everyone believes everyone else's life is perfect. Logically, this makes no sense. But this curated social media existence is real, and it's a real drain.

Most of my mentees tell me that during senior year none of their friends admit to not having a job. This leads those who don't have jobs, which frankly is most of you, to feel alone, and, worse, to fail to seek the help you need since you're not asking for it (for fear of exposing yourself).

Exposing this purported weakness, i.e., saying publicly that you're looking for a job, is hugely beneficial: what you gain in assistance will vastly outweigh the momentary sense of feeling like a failure. Moreover, no one will snicker; most of your peers, in fact, will think you're brave.

Eyes on Your Own Paper, People

Your search process may look different from that of your peers. If you're a history major thinking of joining a think tank, Teach for America or the NSA, it's ridiculously unhelpful to pay attention to your roommate's interview schedule with consulting firms or investment banks. Sure, you'll likely notice a lot of recruiting activity on campus in the fall for finance and consulting positions. But most industries recruit on an ongoing basis and often do so into the spring semester. Pay attention to your goals, and remember that you're likely doing everything you need to do perfectly on time.

Bet on Yourself

Every year, the Fourth of July comes and goes, and most Americans think of fireworks, beer and barbecue. But Independence Day means different things to different people. For the recent college graduates out there, independence, from school, parents, and all that security you've known for the last four years, can be scary. So my wish for all of you is simple: bet on yourselves. Bet that what you've learned about yourself and what you dream of doing are both useful and attainable. Not all in one day, of course. But over the course of the next few years, bet that you can and will make valuable contributions on jobs you care about; this is real independence - from fear.

How Do I Know A Job Is Right For Me?

Self-Knowledge

As my always perceptive friend Matt Harris observed, it's harder for kids these days to develop self-knowledge because they have little time for self-reflection (owing to being over-scheduled). Whether this rings true for you or not, it's indisputable that having self-knowledge is better than not having it.

To start, think about what's going to be meaningful for you. (What have you found meaningful already?) Think about what skills you want to use and develop in your first job after college. Explore options that will help you develop these skills.

Along these lines, I saw some career advice[82] Bucknell put forth for its students. What leapt off the page for me was this:

> "[According to] Executive Director of Career Services Pamela Keiser, 'A student is best able to market themselves when they possess a solid understanding of who they are as an individual. This includes their personality, strengths, skills, experiences, and even their gaps or weaknesses, combined with a keen awareness of what their intended career path or industry seeks and expects of candidates when hiring.'"

This is great advice. What I'd add is one thing: don't wait until April of senior year to begin this self-knowledge process. Start on day 1 of college; adjust as you go, always remembering that this isn't a chore, but a way of later avoiding a job that feels like a chore.

Career Assessment Sites

Multiple assessment services purport to help students uncover jobs that befit their personalities, skills and interests. One is www.careerkey.org.[83] I haven't used this site personally, but anything that gets you thinking hard about your next steps will be helpful.

In a recent New York Times piece, Liz Pearce, CEO of LiquidPlanner described her advice (via her mom, as it were) to new college graduates, "Don't worry about the money, don't worry about the title, don't worry about the company. Just take the job where you can learn the most."

I couldn't agree more. The key then, of course, is how to determine which job will enable you to learn. Some ideas:

---

82 http://bucknellian.net/61036/features/from-campus-to-cubicle-how-you-can-garner-career-worthy-skills-in-college/

83 https://www.careerkey.org/

1. Ask interviewers, as well as older friends already working, about the typical day/week for someone in your position.
2. Ask how much independence you'll have, how you'll be supervised, what is expected for you to know and what you'd do on your own.
3. Ask about the best and worst aspects of their job.
4. Find out the type of person who does well, and who doesn't, at this job.
5. Ask for stories about people who've gotten promoted, and how often young people move from entry-level positions to other posts.
6. Additional, broader questions can be found here.[84]

Please Yourself, Not Anyone Else

Sadly, many recent graduates (and not so recent graduates) take jobs to make their parents happy. Everyone may have each other's best interests in mind, with a shared goal of security knowing that a job has been procured. This article[85] succinctly captures the perils, however, of this approach; read it in full when you can.

Taking a job to please other people almost never works, in the long run. Use your time in college to figure out what you love, and how to translate that into something you do for money. (As long as it's legal, preferably.)

Learn To Love What You Do

Surely discovering a job where you love many of your tasks is a worthy objective. But what if we re-frame doing what you love to loving what you do? Ben Chestnut of Mailchimp (a hugely successful company with almost 3.5 million new users in 2015, according to their annual report), advised as much[86] in a NYT story: "Take the job, learn to live in the moment and love it, master it, and doors will open for you if you're good at what you do. Turn it into a passion if you can."

I don't believe you can "learn to love" accounting if you hated your two accounting classes. I do think, however, that you might learn to love working as a hotel concierge in Milan if you like culture, language, travel and interacting with the public.

---

84 http://www.huffingtonpost.com/julie-kantor/20-professional-discussio_b_12014872.html

85 https://www.nytimes.com/2016/01/03/jobs/a-job-that-nourishes-the-soul-if-not-the-wallet.html?_r=2

86 https://www.nytimes.com/2016/09/04/business/ben-chestnut-of-mailchimp-learn-to-love-the-job-youve-got.html?_r=0

Pick a Field That's Growing

Research the company – and the industry – to determine if it's growing or shrinking. Some seemingly dying fields (like long-form investigative journalism) still can be enticing, though you'll want to at least be aware of the difficulties choosing this route entails. Consider opting instead for industries that obviously need more and more employees. Some that come to mind immediately include physicians' assistants (PA's), anything dealing with elder care, and alternative energy. The climate is clearly changing, and if you choose to believe there's nothing man to do to arrest the potentially catastrophic effects of unfettered climate change, I'm not sure what to say, other than I hope you are an amazing swimmer who doesn't like to eat too much.

In a beautiful commencement speech,[87] John Kerry asserted, "Don't believe the doubters who claim that we have to make a choice between protecting the environment or growing the economy. That's a lie. There are millions of jobs to be created, businesses to be built, fortunes to be made in tapping the potential of renewable energy, and I hope that many of you will share in that future."

This is particularly profound for all those parents worried that robots are taking all the jobs, or that the liberal arts are no longer valuable. Without a world temperate enough for humans, none of the rest of our problems will be important. At a minimum, the opportunities for work in this field are limitless.

Consider Moving

This is a tough notion to get used to, but it must be said: not all of you will be able to live and work at jobs you love in NYC (feel free to replace NYC with another locale that you love).

That said, moving for an enticing job or company can often end up being an amazing experience. And sometimes you'll have no real choice. If you want to be in national politics, or work for a large think tank or lobbyist, Washington D.C. offers tons of opportunities. Want to work for a venture capitalist, or in high tech? Yes, there's more and more of these jobs on the East Coast, but Northern California still dominates this realm. And if your dream is to work in sports, or to be a meteorologist, or as TV/radio person, pack your bags, because Iowa, Maine, and Montana may be where you're headed.

---

87 https://www.c-span.org/video/?408205-1/secretary-state-john-kerry-delivers-commencement-address-northeastern-university

In a December 2016 Fortune article entitled Millennial Innovators Are About to Leave Big Cities,[88] Jason Duff writes, "Fortune 500 companies like Walmart, IBM, Adidas, and Lego all started in small towns. So did billion-dollar startups like Glassdoor, Domo Technologies, Tanium, and SimpliVity. These companies leverage the benefits of small towns (low rent, cheaper employees, less competition), while also leveraging the benefits that only big cities could previously provide (i.e., access to funding through crowdfunding, insights from the world's top entrepreneurs through new media platforms, and tools that make it easier to work virtually.)" While the article tells the story through the lens of entrepreneurs starting the business in far-flung locales, its point for you is still critical: opportunities to do what you want to do, to learn a tremendous amount in a short period of time, and to live in an affordable area, all exist if you're willing to move.

Also on this note is a story from Forbes on 10 cities where recent graduates are finding work and a great quality of life.[89] I admit that Salt Lake City may not be top of mind for most of you (unless you've recently seen the Book of Mormon) but check it out anyway. Many of these cities combine bustling urban areas, replete with bars, sports and the arts, with unmatched affordability.

How To Apply For Jobs

Two methods of applying for jobs exist. The first, which everyone uses, involves applying for known jobs. This includes sending in résumés and cover letters in response to ads you see in places like Ziprecruiter, Indeed, myfirstrealjob.com, simplyhired.com, Craigslist, your school's website and the like, as well as going to interviews with companies that recruit on your campus. (We discussed a lot of this in Chapter 12.) You may be taking advantage of the alert feature many of these sites offer, allowing you to become aware of new jobs as soon as they are posted. There's nothing "wrong" with this approach, as long as this isn't your only move.

The second, under-used tactic is what I call creating a job: identifying companies for which you'd like to work, and then, regardless of whether they seem to have any open positions, contacting those entities and establishing a dialogue.

I'm not going to spend a lot of time here repeating the techniques outlined in previous chapters. Instead, let's focus on approach number two.

---

88 http://fortune.com/2016/12/21/millennials-cities/
89 http://www3.forbes.com/leadership/the-top-10-up-and-coming-cities-for-recent-college-grads-2/2/

Step One: Pinpoint Your Target Companies

This entire book is designed to help you with this very thing, the identification of companies for which you'd like to work. Now research these companies' websites. It's possible that jobs actually might be posted here. Additionally, you can learn the types of jobs that exist in that company, information that is not always intuitive.

Never Overlook the Obvious

In one of my earliest days at my first job, I noticed that a co-worker seemed frustrated. I asked what was up, and learned that he'd been looking for days for a particular person he needed to interview regarding a person we were researching. I went to the big bookshelf where we stored phone books, among other things, and found the person immediately, right there, listed in the book. (Yes, prior to Google, there was an actual book containing names, addresses and numbers for every area of the country. In fact, older editions were treasures. This probably makes as much sense to you students as the fact that we used to have get up to change a TV channel manually. After we got done feeding our pet dinosaurs.)

How does this translate to you? Use your school's network. Your school's alumni are all over the world and work in a variety of industries. While not all of them will respond to your requests for insight, many will, simply owing to the shared school connection (along with a well-crafted note). Not reaching out to alumni for career guidance guarantees that you won't get rejected. It also guarantees that you'll get no help.

Use your school's intranet site (ask Career Services for help here) and LinkedIn to identify alumni that interest you, based on what they do and where they work. LinkedIn has what it terms an "advanced" search. You enter in a target company, along with the name of your school, and it kicks back a list of people who meet both criteria. You can refine this further by specifying that you only are interested in people who went to your school and who still work at a certain firm. To narrow the results even more, you can add other things, too, like geographical preferences and job titles.

Once you've gathered your list, craft an email clearly outlining who you are and what you're hoping to accomplish with this person. The following is a template you can use; naturally, you'll adjust it according to your own interests. (One particularly effective method is to specify products/ brands and companies that have captured your attention. Explain that you're looking to work in a certain field for one of these brands or companies, or other similar brands and companies.)

Hello <u>abc</u>,

My name is <u>xxx</u> and I saw from LinkedIn that you are a fellow (fill in your school's mascot's name).

I'm a <u>grade</u> at school, majoring in <u>aaaaa</u> and minoring in <u>bbbb</u>, and I'm very interested in the <u>fill in the appropriate</u> industry.

I've been fascinated by <u>name of industry/company or even product</u> for a long time from a consumer standpoint, and more recently I've decided to get more involved from the business or even <u>design</u> aspect. I'd love to have the opportunity to pursue more <u>industry</u>-related vocational pursuits while I'm in <u>the town or city where you'd like to go</u> for this semester, and I'd also especially love the chance to work in <u>industry</u> when I graduate in <u>month</u>.
Would you be available to talk about this on the phone at some point this week? I'm free between 3:00 and 5:00 pm this <u>Thursday</u>, as well after 11 am on <u>Friday</u>. Also, I'd be totally happy to just communicate over email if you'd prefer!

Thank you so much and I look forward to hearing from you.

Best,

Your name

Ultimately, you'll need to convince your potential employer both why you're interested in that particular job and why you're capable of doing that particular job. Keep this thought fresh when drafting your emails.

Six Degrees of Separation
As mentioned in both Chapter 10 and Chapter 12, you don't know who in your network knows someone who can assist you, until you ask.

As with the LinkedIn and School Intranet idea, you'll first create a list of all the adults you know, including your relatives, your parents' friends, your friends' parents, your professors, your former bosses, etc.

Using a slightly different version of the above template, you'll blast out an email to your list. (DO NOT have your parents send it on your behalf. This isn't a playdate being organized for you when you were five. Few things reflect worse on a college student than parents speaking for them.) You'll explain what you're looking for, and ask for any help your network can provide. It's very likely that some percentage of these people will know other people who can help you.

Cold Emails Can Lead to Hot Leads

The aforementioned Ian Bullard, a senior at Rutgers as of this writing, clued me in to the idea that cold emails can result in amazing connections. Ian has reached out to people with whom he has no previous ties. Utilizing an email that is both deferential and attention-grabbing, he's gotten responses from a number of leading executives of large companies.

This technique augments the more "connected" ideas discussed above. Many people are tempted to dismiss it because it's uncomfortable. Don't.

Spreadsheets Are Boring, But Effective

Given how many entities you'll be tracking, some form of a spreadsheet will become necessary to keep track of who you've reached and where you are with each target entity. Include the name of the company (obviously), who you contacted, how you know that person, their email address, their cell number, when you are scheduled to meet or follow up, and what they've told you.

It doesn't really matter whether you go old school and use Excel, or avail yourself of a higher-tech, cloud-based solution. Just do something.

Social Media Isn't Just for Killing Time

Finally you can tell your parents that spending time on your phone and computer isn't just you goofing off. Using Facebook, LinkedIn, Twitter, Snapchat, Instagram, Google alerts and whatever else comes on the scene, follow all of the companies you're pursuing. You may be fortunate to learn of a job opening before the company posts it on a site like Indeed. More likely, you'll discover news you can use to establish a dialogue with people at the company, some of whom may find a spot for you even if no specific job opening existed. At a minimum, you'll learn about a field that is attractive to you, something that will help you in your preparation for job interviews.

Network Spin

We've touched on the idea of compellingly telling your story to those who ask, rather than being dismissive because you're nervous or frustrated.

A June 2015 Bloomberg story[90] mentioned a concise and dynamic method for overcoming these nerves and frustrations:

> If you've recently completed college or grad school and are searching for a job, there are two questions you've probably come to dread: 'What do you do?' and the related follow-up, 'What do you want to do with your life?'

> These questions are usually asked by parents, friends, and other well-meaning people trying to take an interest in you. More often than not, the questions just stress you out. You feel embarrassed if you haven't locked down a job, and you feel judged if you don't have an airtight explanation of how you want to spend the next two or three decades.

> At this point in your life, it truly is difficult to answer the question of what you want to do. You're not in a position to know the full range of jobs, or even the possible directions that might appeal to you .... But getting this right is an essential part of a winning job search strategy. Remember that over half of all job offers are the result of referrals, so you need these polite questioners to advocate for you and suggest you for opportunities. Having a compelling and concise 'elevator pitch' – a speech that could be contained in a short elevator ride— is the way you'll hook them.

---

90 https://www.bloomberg.com/news/articles/2015-06-23/two-sentences-that-will-help-you-get-the-job-you-want

Summing yourself up in a couple of seconds shouldn't intimidate you. There is a simple formula for figuring out what you should say. ... Be ready to deliver a two-sentence summary that will give people an idea of who you are [the hook], what you're interested in [the frame], and what you've done in the past [the support]. The goal is that when the person you're speaking with comes across a potentially valuable connection or opportunity that could be right for you, your name will leap to mind."

Some elevator pitches that embody the frame, support and hook are below.

"I'm interested in government work and am considering law school. I'm exploring paralegal opportunities and Congressional internships to test this out."

"I'm passionate about the environment, so I'm looking at nonprofits that fight global warming and other environmental hazards."

"I've always loved the stock market, so I'm looking at a wide variety of opportunities in finance and investing."

Practice your answer until you can recite it from memory. When you meet people in an elevator, or off of one, you'll be ready.

Turn Failure into Success

The aforementioned Reshma Saujani, Founder and Chief Executive of Girls Who Code, gave a powerful TED talk, entitled "Teach Girls Bravery, Not Perfection," available here.[91] The title says it all, but listen to the talk, too.

As indicated above, the problem with no one sharing their failures is not only do people feel alone in their troubles, but also that no one gets the help that others can and want to provide. It's not fun to make mistakes, but it's normal and incredibly energizing to learn from them. What's more, it humanizes you to those around you. Speaking about your own mistakes makes you vulnerable; those close to you will want to help you overcome these errors as a natural reaction to that vulnerability. (If they

---

91 https://www.ted.com/talks/reshma_saujani_teach_girls_bravery_not_perfection

don't, they're probably not the friends you thought they were, which is disappointing but good to know.)

Differentiate, Don't Compete

Based on conversations I've had with students, both current and former, as well as with professors and college administrators, it seems that many college career centers have a different agenda than the students have. Much of this isn't the career office's fault. With corporate counsel looking over their shoulder, they need to minimize risks. This means not advising students kids to go off the beaten path and instead taking a middle of the road approach with everyone. The goal for the college is to be able to say that students are graduating with a job that ostensibly is in "their field." It doesn't really matter what job this is. (Individual stories lead me to conclude that individual career counselors and professors veer even further, cajoling students to study a certain field like accounting or to take higher paying jobs, even if those don't fit the student's aptitudes and interests, to boost the college's earnings average.)

Amongst the problems with this philosophy is that it leads students to compete with one another for the same few jobs and by doing the same exact things. I know a professor of health studies at a prestigious university; he was a medical doctor prior to joining academia. A student approached him in a panic about medical school. It seems the student thus far had been unable to secure a summer job in a hospital or in medical research. All he had found, in fact, was a job at a flower shop. The professor listened and told him something he anticipated the career office would never say: take the florist job. The professor surmised that the medical school would receive thousands of applications, all from students who'd had summer jobs in medicine. How many would they read from someone who'd worked as a florist? One. In his mind, differentiating oneself is far easier than competing with the masses. It certainly seems risky and won't work for every field. But when you have the opportunity to learn real skills and develop a fascinating story, take it.

Screw Your Title

Executive Assistant - yuck. Administrative Assistant - crap. Temp - the worst. These titles send shudders through some recent college graduates, who think, "I didn't go to college to be someone's assistant, or worse, to be a temp." Here's the thing: In many industries, these assistant/temp jobs are the EXACT JOB you need to take if you want to break in to that industry. If that's the case, just think of this job, crappy title and all, as your big opportunity (which it is), rather than a failure (which it isn't). What you learn and who you meet are far more important than what you are called.

Beating the Machines

To beat mechanical résumé screeners, I advise going around them, rather than through them. As alluded to above, instead of just applying to ads you see on various job sites, go first to the social media pages of companies that intrigue you. In a *Business News Daily* piece, Leah Paul, director of marketing at Mediabistro, noted, "In addition to a presence on LinkedIn, most big companies have dedicated recruiting accounts on Twitter or Facebook[92] that post job openings. 'Lots of smaller companies and startups might not have a careers page or even a dedicated recruiting team, so an alternative is to go to your favorite job board and set up a job alert. … If you don't have any target companies, but know what you want to be doing, conduct your searches on keywords and phrases that speak to the responsibilities you hope to have in your next role. Or search for the qualifications you have."

Other ideas for meeting humans, rather than trying to defeat machines, come from *IT World*. Jack Martin, founder and CEO of Technology Jobs NYC, asserted, "The best way to get around gatekeepers is to meet informally prior to discussing any potential jobs," he says. "There are countless ways to approach a potential employer on a personal level and develop a strong dialogue before any professional discussion begins. This can be achieved by attending networking events, socials, or even just sending a quick 'hello' on LinkedIn.[93] Stay out of the black hole of electronic HR by forming a human connection first."

How To Accept … Or Reject An Offer

Accepting offers seems like a simple procedure. Still, I've seen and heard of some stumbles that illustrate what to do, based on what not to do.

---

92 http://www.businessnewsdaily.com/9358-digital-job-search-guide.html

93 http://www.itworld.com/article/2877257/get-your-resume-past-the-robots-how-to-beat-hrs-mechanical-gatekeepers.html#slide6

A friend related a story about a younger relative (we'll call her Sarah), who was graduating college in a few months and looking for a job on the West Coast (where her friend was going to work), though she lives on the East Coast. Sarah was interested in marketing and my friend has a lot of contacts in the industry. Within one hour of speaking about it, Sarah had an interview which led to a job offer at a mid-sized marketing company. She accepted the offer. About one month prior to the job's start date, my friend received a call from Sarah's mother saying that Sarah's friend wasn't able to go out west and so Sarah no longer wanted the job. She thanked my friend for her help and hung up.

Unpacking this story, we discover a few (burnt) kernels of data. For starters, my friend's relative somehow expected her to contact the employer to let them know Sarah wouldn't be showing up; this obviously is preposterous and incredibly juvenile. More significantly, Sarah had made a commitment to an entity that was counting on her. There are situations where employers, usually super large companies, will make offers to loads of students early in the year, and make it clear that while they want people who accept to actually join the firm come May, they understand (like colleges) that only a percentage of the acceptances will turn into hires. This situation did not fit that category; Sarah did a great disservice to the employer by reneging on her agreement.

I also got an email from a friend describing a similar scenario:

"At any given time, I employ a handful of young [people]. I find it challenging to work with most of them (they often exhibit some or all of the following traits: irresponsible, entitled, non-communicative, disrespectful, unreliable, unprofessional). Every so often, there's one that stands out. Last year, it was [Ashley – whose name I have changed]. She's a sweet, energetic, young woman who communicated well and was reliable. She was working for me while finishing up her Masters. Ashley is a great employee, passionate about her work and eager to improve. ... Ashley was seeking a full-time job as a Phys Ed teacher in a school. After many interviews, she accepted a job she was excited about starting several months later. As it turned out, about 6 weeks later, Ashley got another job offer that she preferred. When she told me, I asked her how she was going to handle it and she told me she didn't know but she was really uncomfortable and nervous to tell the woman at the job she accepted. Of course she was! We talked about possible dialogue and I even had her role play. When I saw Ashley the following week, I asked her how it went and she told me she wound up emailing the woman because it was easier. I was speechless. The woman later wrote her to say that she is happy that this happened because they would never want someone in their employ who exercised such poor judgment and was so unprofessional. I couldn't agree more!"

When you're looking for your first job, you may be fortunate enough to end up with competing offers, though not always simultaneously. If you receive an offer and are hoping for another, accept the risk that delaying a response to company one may cause them to hire someone else instead. If you do receive offer two, be honest with company one. A simple statement goes a long way: "Thank you. I enjoyed learning about your company but I have another opportunity that I think is right for me at this time."

In another example of what not to do, this time involving salary negotiations, a friend was hiring a recent graduate I had referred to him. After some back and forth about the starting salary, I thought an agreement had been reached, one that would please both parties. Then my friend sent me the following email, which he'd received from the candidate:

Hi xxx,

Yes, I saw your email thank you. I need to discuss the new offer with my parents as both they and I still have concerns about the feasibility of this arrangement. As it did not meet our minimum criteria, I will get back to you after the weekend.

The pattern I hope readers are seeing emerge here is the use of parents as surrogates in the job hunt. I certainly encourage parents to discuss job offers your children receive. Overruling an offer that has been discussed and accepted, however, is discouraged. As for students, remember all of the things we've talked about in this book. If a job sounds exciting because of the tasks involved, and you are confident you'll learn a multitude of transferable skills, and the money is adequate for your needs, then accepting makes perfect sense. Beyond that, be extremely leery about accepting and then going back on this. Furthermore, citing your parents in an email to a future employer signals immaturity, which definitely not the message you want to send. (The post script to the above story is hugely positive, as the student did join the company and every day is rewarding the company's patience with excellent work.)

How To Act At Work

How to act on a job is something most people take for granted, but entry level workers can find befuddling. Let's review some stuff that should ease the transition from fun/partying (oops- I mean, working hard in college) to the so-called real world.

Set Your Alarm

Showing up ready to work means that at 9am, or whenever you are supposed to start your day, you actually start your day. It doesn't mean you come in and spend 20 minutes updating your fantasy baseball roster or checking out twitter while drinking your morning cup of mocha latte. It's true that you might not get "caught," at first, but trust me, when you do (and you will, eventually), you'll make someone important look at you quite differently.

Whatever you need to do to get to work on time, do it. If you notice a train will get you in 10 minutes before your start time, and it's a five minute walk from the train to the office, be aware that this is cutting things mighty close. Take the earlier train. Being the person known for being early is not a "waste of time;" it's an investment in your work reputation.

Dress the Way Your Colleagues Do

As anyone who ever saw me on the way to work knows, my company never cared about dress codes. Most companies still do, however. The fastest way to draw negative attention to yourself is showing up under-dressed by your employer's standards.

How do you prevent this? If you didn't notice the way people were dressed during your interview(s), as awkward as it sounds the best thing to do is to simply ask for guidance from the person offering you a job when the offer is presented. If that opportunity passes, call and ask your interviewer, HR (if the company is big enough), or really anyone who picks up, what the company dress code entails.

Two seconds of discomfort is well worth the comfort of being appropriately attired.

Be Nice

Be nice, not just to your boss, but to everyone. Do it because it's the right thing to do: the security guard and cleaning person are people who have earned respect, just like the CEO and your supervisor. And do it for self-preservation: People talk; if you're a jerk to an assistant she may inform people who are important to your career. Moreover, someone may see your behavior, which would reflect poorly on you. Be a mensch (simply put, do the right thing).

Pay Attention During Training

You've gotten to work on time and ready to go. You're dressed well. The next step? Some kind of training/orientation, right? Unlike college, though, when some people (not those reading this, obviously) would be tempted to play on their phones and not pay attention at all to another boring training seminar, work is different.

PUT YOUR PHONE AWAY AND BRING A NOTEPAD. Nerdy? Perhaps, but there's nothing more irksome to an employer than an employee who asks the same question repeatedly, especially one that was answered in training (more on this below).

The upside of a notepad, as opposed to the multitude of online systems (Google Keep, Evernote, Stickies for Mac, Tumblr, Wordpress, or even a Calendar app), is that you can take notes while still maintaining eye contact with your supervisor. You can always go back later and enter your notes into a searchable system, but when you take them on a computer, it tends to be distracting.

Ask Questions ...Just Not the Same Ones

Asking questions at work doesn't make you stupid; not asking questions, then doing your job poorly, certainly will. Here's a great quote from a recent *New York Times* story,[94] "Research shows that question-asking peaks at age 4 or 5, as children pass through school (where answers are often more valued than questions) ... By the time we're in the workplace, many of us have gotten out of the habit of asking fundamental questions about what's going on around us."

94 https://www.nytimes.com/2016/07/03/jobs/the-power-of-why-and-what-if.html?_r=1

Don't be this way. After being trained, new employees often realize they're expected to know a lot of information, but aren't quite sure what to do when, well, they don't know something. This is where your notebook comes into play. Businesses will always want you to ask questions; they just don't want you asking the same questions every day.

Ask Questions by Presenting Solutions

More than simply asking questions, it's how you frame your questions that counts.

Here's a classic question from a new salesperson: "What do I do when a client calls and asks me a question I don't know how to answer?"

Seems like a reasonable request, right?

But what if the employee presented it like this, instead:

"If a client calls and asks me a question I don't know how to answer, I think I'd say that, 'I don't know, but I'll get back to you shortly after discussing it with my colleagues.' Would that be the right response?'"

Now as an employer, I hear my new salesman taking initiative by offering a potential solution AS WELL AS seeking counsel regarding her judgment, both of which portend future success, and both of which make me confident that I made the right decision hiring her.

Ask Why

The aforementioned New York Times article related the story behind Polaroid[95] (which for those who don't know, invented a camera that produced instantly developed pictures). According to the article, "The inspiration for the instant camera sprang from a question asked in the mid-1940s by the 3-year-old daughter of its inventor, Edwin H. Land. She was impatient to see a photo her father had just snapped, and when he tried to explain that the film had to be processed first, she wondered aloud, "Why do we have to wait for the picture?"

Ask why your employer does things the way they do. Who knows, you might just contribute to a whole new way of doing things.

---

95 https://www.nytimes.com/2016/07/03/jobs/the-power-of-why-and-what-if.html?_r=0

Be Proactive

If step one is asking questions, step two is asking them the right way, and step three is asking why, then the final step might be asking questions at the right time.

Here I'm going to quote one of the best supervisors and employee trainers I've ever seen, Jen Callahan. Jen worked with me at BackTrack, the investigative shop I founded. (Jen's also an enormously talented mimic, but that's a side of her that few people see, sadly. Break it out more, Jen, for all of our benefit.)

When I asked Jen for her thoughts on how new employees should act at work, this was her reply, "OK, here's my novel-length input about how to act, beyond the typical 'show up on time' and 'put your ass in the chair and actually work.'"

"It's important to give the impression that you want to please and quickly get good at what you were hired to do. Be proactive about learning your duties: If you complete a task, but aren't sure if it was fully done correctly, ask someone. Say, "I did X, Y and Z to complete this task, are those all the steps?" Compare this to the employee who does the exact same steps and then sits at his desk surfing the Internet and waits for someone to come over and say, "When you did that task, you only did X, Y and Z and forgot step Q." I always tired quickly when the latter scenario would happen and a new employee would say, "Oh, I didn't know Q was part of it." It's true the employee didn't know about Q, but also this person didn't bother to confirm whether or not the task had been done correctly. As we almost always trained in groups, it was telling to see who seemed to care that they were doing things right, and asked upfront, versus those who seemed satisfied with whatever effort they put forth and waited on others to correct them."

You Are Not the Boss

Temper your expectations. You are not the boss on day 1, and you won't be the boss on day 2 either. Your first two years of work, in fact, are more like your 5th and 6th years of college, but with you getting paid instead of you and/or your parents paying huge sums to your school.

You are at work to learn and to be valuable to your employer. You will not make them money initially; they have to train you, which costs them time and money, and then put up with your mistakes and relatively low production. In return, you'll dedicate yourself to becoming an asset as fast as you can, and then commit to this company until you've learned all you can.

Mary Barra, Chairman and CEO of General Motors (GM), commented in a LinkedIn piece[96] on how GM hires, "We want a team that's eager to learn, lead and inspire other people to excel in a variety of domains – because change is constant. The auto industry will be radically different just five short years from now, so we're looking for people who have built a portfolio of experiences rather than just worrying about the next promotion."

Do this, and you'll have earned money, pride, transferrable skills and a great reference.

Patience

As alluded to above, your path to becoming a top executive (should that be your goal) won't be a short one. Be patient. In your first job, things take time. We may indeed be in an instant gratification era but recognize that it takes time to meet colleagues, to feel busy and to feel like you're adding value.

While you don't want to be permanently complacent, being in a rush to achieve all of these things will be counter-productive. If you do notice that you're often sitting around with nothing to do, absolutely approach your boss and colleagues and ask if there's anything you can do to help. If that fails, set up a coffee chat with a supervisor and constructively discuss how you can be better utilized. Make it about the company. "I want to do more because I'm bored" is nice, but a little childish. Replace that with, "I'm hoping to do more to help us produce a better product/service; what do you suggest?"

Indispensable

Why make yourself indispensable? Think of this process as both a short and long term investment. Short term, by learning everything about many roles in your company, you'll be less likely to lose your job, and more likely to earn a promotion. You'll also uncover talents and interests you may not have known you had. Long term, you'll be able to use these skills at every job you have in the future.

Your ability to learn how various roles in your company function might be constrained by your day-to-day tasks and your level of access to company data. What's

---

96 https://www.linkedin.com/pulse/how-i-hire-people-who-arent-like-you-other-tricks-weve-mary-barra

more, what's best for you and your future must still also be best for your company; they're not likely to encourage you to learn skills that don't benefit them too.

One way of ensuring that everyone's interests are aligned is to volunteer to solve problems, either one you've identified, or one put forth by management. Volunteer to do things – especially stuff you know how to do – even if it's "not your job." Fix the computer tech system. Rework the company's Snapchat and other social media profiles. Edit the training manual based on your own training experience.

Do more than is asked of you. This takes patience, good judgment, and the ability to develop rapport with your co-workers (which itself requires listening skills and a strong emotional quotient – your EQ). Like interviewing, writing or most anything else, all of these skills can be learned, and with conscious and consistent practice, they'll become natural.

Here's an example from Jen C.:

"Pay attention to and learn how the organization functions. It's not just about 'What am I required to do?' and 'What are my specific job functions?' but also, 'What could I do?' If you have free time and your boss is busy (and therefore going to the boss for work isn't a great idea), rather than relaxing, ask a colleague - anyone on your level or below, if there is below you - if they could use help. In my first after-college job I had VERY few responsibilities. I was going crazy, so I literally walked around to everyone else at the organization and said, 'Hey, do you need any help with anything at all?' Only one person ever really took me up on the offer, but at least I had something to do and he liked having the help. It was also illustrative because I found that most others weren't doing much, either, and I [therefore] got out of there as quickly as I could."

Another example was given to me by a friend who wished to remain anonymous:

"I did an internship at a newspaper during college and the people there were extremely cool, except for one guy, who was a pain in the ass. There were 5 interns that fall and one day in early October the intern supervisor called me in and said the other 4 interns had refused to work with this guy. She asked me if I would still work with this guy and I said of course I would. I still can't believe the other interns did that. It's 4 months of your life and we were only there 3 days a week. Yes, this man was condescending, disorganized and not especially intelligent. Yes, he would give me a task and after I completed it, he'd realize he really wanted something else and I'd start over. But who cares? It's not like I had all this other work to do. And so many of the other employees at the paper would empathize with me about him – they'd make jokes about him when he wasn't around, etc., and I suspect they might not have talked to me at all if they didn't see me dealing with him. I also suspect I got a couple of my coolest assignments from people who watched me work with him and keep my cool."

Advocate ... Without Sounding Spoiled

Advocating means speaking up when you believe you have something of value to offer your company. It doesn't mean saying you cannot work on a Friday in the summer because you're going to a beach house; this time off you have to ask for, in advance. It can be unnatural and unnerving to speak up when you've learned that putting your head down and remaining silent is generally satisfactory behavior. Sometimes, however, this isn't enough. Say you're working on social media marketing and you notice that your company tweets only infrequently. You know that tweeting more often, along with following numerous other accounts, has a better chance of upping your profile. Bring this up to your manager, in private, and ask to help if no one else is available. At worst, you'll be told no. But you might just jump start your career this way, and certainly this is a productive habit to develop.

Be Open to Change

In an April 2015 *Absolute Return* article, Jason Karp of Tourbillon Capital (a hedge fund) said that he had hired a former CIA interrogator to administer a "three-step personality exam" to "dig deeper into the personality traits of new hires." Mr. Karp was quoted as follows: "One of the things we screen for, that shows up on all of the professionals that we hire, is a variable called 'openness to change.' It is the single most important variable we screen for." The piece reported that Mr. Karp divides potential job candidates into three categories: excellent, dangerous and nuisance; per Mr. Karp, excellent candidates possess both "openness to change" and "grit", while dangerous candidates "are those who are 'so brilliant that they think everything they believe is correct.'"

The most successful employees I've seen were those who got better all the time. Being open to change fosters this process. Obviously, this process requires you to accept criticism, which can be difficult for people. Fear of making mistakes and suffering the dreaded bruised ego can get in the way of listening, learning and changing. It's easier to stay the same, even if that is ineffective, because making mistakes is embarrassing. But this is only true if you define mistakes this way, as opposed to being opportunities to improve.

Mistakes and Weaknesses are Fine. Burdening Others with Them Isn't

More from Jen C:

> "A tale of two investigators, each hired off the street and each who got a lot of 'repeat edit' edits (by way of explanation, Jen is referring to her editing this person's work, only to repeat the same type of edit in the next report the person wrote): Employee #1 never seemed frustrated with his poor work or apologetic about it; his edits were arduous and time-consuming, but he never seemed to make many adjustments to his process; he rarely responded to emails from superiors quickly (sometimes took 20 minutes or more, and we had to talk to him about this several times); and would come in at 9:20AM or leave at 4:45PM sometimes. When this person, after approximately two months, got an inkling that things weren't going well, he asked me what I thought about his performance. I told him truthfully and he got defensive and said, 'Well, how am I expected to learn so much so quickly?' [The] answer, of course, is by putting in the effort. Contrast that with Employee #2, who was at her desk every morning before 9AM, and never rushed out the door at the end of the day; who responded to emails quickly 100% of the time; and who proactively addressed the 're-peat edit' problem by reaching out to me, apologizing for repeating the mistake, explaining how she'd been trying to avoid the edit and asking if there was something else she could be doing. Employee #1 was a flameout

prior to three months, and Employee #2 is well on the way to being a good investigator."

Being Good is Your Responsibility

Yes, it's true. Getting good at your job is actually on you. Naturally it's more effective for a company to train you, and to provide manuals and guidelines for you to refer to and follow. Ultimately, though, becoming a valuable employee is up to you. A good example of what not to do comes from Jen C.: "Never say in training, 'Boy, you guys are really going to have to hammer me on that one – that's gonna be tough for me to adjust to.' I've heard this several times and it's a strike against the person because, um, this is your job and you are responsible for your performance." Yep. Strike one. Two more and it'll be time to dust off your résumé.

Your Co-Workers' Business is Just That – Their Business

One of the thorniest jobs for managers is navigating all of the egos and hopes of their team of employees. Part of this is ameliorated by keeping employees' pay a secret; we've seen the jealousy and controversy that occurs in professional sports, where payroll information is public. Bigger problems stem, however, from perceived (or real) differences in how one employee is treated, compared to other members of the staff. Your job is to pay attention to your own work, and trust that this will result in you getting what you need. Here's a story illustrating how this happens, as described by Jen C:

> "It doesn't matter what others are doing or getting, it matters how well you are doing. I've looked at some of the reviews ... and there was talk of managers having 'favorites.' This kills me. Show up and do excellent work, and you're going to be a favorite. It's that simple. The only people who complain about the preferential treatment they perceive others are getting are people who aren't producing and who therefore aren't getting rhythm in any other areas. Employee #1 is very conscientious, polite, punctual, hardworking and extremely productive. Edits go quickly, and he produced a large volume of work even in his early weeks of employment. Employee #1 also has a long commute and family out of state who he likes to visit on weekends. This person asked and was allowed to work from home on certain Fridays/Mondays early in his tenure. He's not a 'favorite;' he's an excellent worker who was writing twice as

many reports as would be normal for his experience level. Employee #2, who was hired alongside Employee #1, should not and did not concern himself with this. Employee #2 was aware that learning the job was difficult for him, and his commute was not long. Therefore, he came to the office every day, got to know his colleagues and kept his head down and worked, if much slower than Employee #1. Employee #2, by the end of three months, was on his way to getting good at the job. If he had distracted himself with stories in his head about how 'They like the other guy better than me,' then he might have derailed his own growth and needlessly reduced his satisfaction with the job."

Along these lines, refrain from discussing your pay. No good ever comes of this. Either you're upset that someone got a better deal than you, or vice versa. Especially on your first job, sweating your pay in comparison to others is poor form. Take what you can live on and what the market will bear, and be happy for the opportunity to work and earn.

Knowledge Beats Ignorance
It won't kill you to pay attention to news about your company. Follow them on social media. Read a newspaper. Depending on the size of the firm, you may even want to set up a Google Alert to ping you when the firm is mentioned publicly. If you're in the marketing department, I'd consider doing this regarding competitors as well. If a competitor makes a big announcement about a new product line, or a top executive leaves, you probably want to know about it. It certainly won't hurt.

Your Computer isn't Yours, and Your Usage isn't Private
I like to view things through the upside/downside prism. If there's no upside to an activity, but the downside is considerable (even if the chances of this downside occurring are small), don't do that activity.

On a job, this means:

1. Limit your viewing of non-work websites, and certainly never look at inappropriate sites on your work computer or work phone. Recognize that this usage can be tracked.

2. Similarly, be very careful what you say using a work email address. Don't re-send inappropriate jokes to your buddies. Tell them to use your personal email address if they insist on sending you stuff. Watch your sarcasm, which doesn't always register properly in an email. (Emails, remember, are permanent.) Think of it this way: would you be happy if your comments were printed in a newspaper?

How To Leave A Job

Leaving a job is never easy. The trick is in knowing when it's time. One method I suggest is reviewing whether you've learned all you're going to at your job, and more importantly, at your company. Have you truly mastered the tasks you do perform? Have you approached your supervisor and asked for additional tasks? Have you asked whether there are other jobs within the firm that might need filling, and where your skills would fit? If you can answer yes to all these questions, and if the responses were yes, no and no, it might be time to start looking.

Consider that it is usually better to look for a job when you already have one; the longer you are out of work, the more likely a potential new employer may think this has something to do with you, rather than the job market. The exception is if you work a tremendous amount of hours. In that case, finding another job may be impossible given your time constraints. Still, it'll be best to at least map out a search strategy before you leave.

If you do leave, always do so on good terms, if at all possible. Explain why you are leaving, and express gratitude for the opportunities you were given. Offer to stay on if that would help the company transition your role to someone else. Say goodbye, in person, to your colleagues. And don't criticize the company or your boss on your future interviews.

Homework

1. Spend two to three focused hours every day on your search. Try doing so at different times of day, and measure the results.

2. Each day, set up at least two calls or coffee meetings with adults in your prospective field. Create a city day; wherever you live, plan a day to meet four to five people in the city nearest to you.

3. Treat your network like a winter holiday fire. The more you feed it, the more it grows.

4. Think about trying to land your first job the way a good cook thinks about a meal. First, the cook figures out what people might enjoy eating, whether it's ethnic cuisine, spicy food or vegetarian dishes. Next he shops for ingredients. Then the prepping happens – slicing, dicing, marinating, etc. Only when all these steps have been taken does the actual "cooking" take place.

5. Once you land a job, your notebook is your best friend. When senior people talk, start writing.

6. Take joy and pride in your work; smile every day.

Getting any job is not a goal. Getting a job you want is.

CHAPTER 16

Resources

I t seems like every day I come across another website, blog or book that speaks to the college experience. The following list is thus not in any way exhaustive. Reading any or all of these materials will undoubtedly be useful, some more for parents, others for students, and many for both. Enjoy.

Books

Designing your Life, Bill Burnett and Dave Evans

Strength Finder, Tom Rath

To Sell is Human, Daniel Pink

48 Laws of Power, Robert Greene

Overloaded and Underprepared: Strategies for Stronger Schools and Healthy, Successful Kids by Dennis Pope and Maureen Brown

Cut the Crap, Get a Job!: A New Job Search Process for a New Era by Dana Manciagli

The Blessing of a B Minus: Using Jewish Teachings to Raise Resilient Teenagers by Wendy Mogul

How to Raise an Adult: Break Free of the Overparenting Trap and Prepare Your Kid for Success by Julie Lythcott-Haims

I Could Do Anything If I Only Knew What it Was: How to Discover What You Really Want and How to Get It by Barbara Sher

What Color is Your Parachute by Richard Nelson Bolles

Where You Go Is Not Who You'll Be: An Antidote to the College Admissions Mania by Frank Bruni

Aspiring Adults Adrift by Richard Arum and Josipa Roksa

There Is Life After College: What Parents and Students Should Know About Navigating School to Prepare for the Jobs of Tomorrow *by Jeffrey Selingo (scheduled for release by HarperCollins in the spring of 2016)*

The Gift of Failure: How the Best Parents Learn to Let Go So Their Children Can Succeed by Jessica Lahey

Moving to College: What to Do, What to Learn, What to Pack by Helene Tragos Stelian

Other sources

Pathways to College Online Library[97] A college and career readiness guide, all in one website, geared to under-privileged students especially

The New York Times Sunday Business Section, Corner Office column

One on One Mentors Facebook page[98]

---

97 http://www.pathwaylibrary.org/ListTopics.aspx

98 https://www.facebook.com/oneononecollegementors/

CHAPTER 17

Conclusion

T hose of you who've made it this far are undoubtedly praying this final chapter is brief. (When writing it, I was thinking the same thing.) With this in mind, I have a few final thoughts I need to convey. Here goes.

Why Write This Book at All?

I described my background in the Introduction to this book. I mentioned that I'd helped hire and train hundreds of employees for over two decades. What I omitted is that the process of training young employees and watching them develop their skills and their voices was easily the most gratifying part of the work for me.

When I was approached by my alma mater, Rutgers University, to participate in their mentoring program, I thought, "Finally, a place to get back to doing what I really want to do." That initial experience spawned One on One Mentors, which as of the publication of this book has me mentoring nearly 20 students, and loving every moment of it.

I'm incredibly eager to see you transform your time at college. I'm very hopeful I can contribute to that, even in a small way. And I'm most looking forward to seeing the results – witnessing you emerge from school confident in your abilities to procure work that is meaningful to you. I hope this book demonstrated my intentions.

College goes by in a flash. Maximizing your time there requires slowing it down. You do that by establishing a plan. Not a plan that you never deviate from, but a plan that provides structure to your four years.

Are Coaching and Mentoring Euphemisms for Coddling?

If done poorly, I suppose coaching can turn into doing things for students that you should be doing yourselves. But saying that all coaching and mentoring is akin to coddling is like thinking that a good trainer at the gym coddles you. A good trainer, like a good mentor, inspires you to do more than you thought you could. A good trainer pushes you past your uncomfortable points. A good trainer watches your technique, and helps you adjust it accordingly. And a good trainer holds you accountable for doing what you said you'd do. A good trainer doesn't do your push-ups for you, and no trainer ultimately can "make" you come to the gym.

A good mentor does all this and more. A good mentor introduces you to adults who can help you. A good mentor helps you determine what you're skilled at doing. A good mentor guides your self-evaluation of your interests. A good mentor works with you as your skills and interests evolve over time, encouraging you to embrace these changes, rather than be fearful of them. A good mentor shows you how real confidence is derived from you accomplishing actual results, rather than merely showing up. A good mentor helps you persevere. A good mentor also teaches practical skills, from how to interact with adults to how to handle yourself in an interview. A good mentor customizes what he's providing based on what you need. A good mentor is part cheerleader, part nudge, part psychologist, part trainer, and part job expert. Finally, a good mentor facilitates your understanding of how your skills and interests connect to you getting a job you want post-graduation.

As my lovely wife Michelle once said, "The mentor provides the seeds to plant. But the students have to dig the hole."

My always insightful sister Shelley emailed me the following synopsis. "I heard a lecture once from a psychologist who stated that career success is heavily driven by your ability to use your resources to learn what you don't know. You'll never know everything, but you have to always know how to figure out what you don't know — by utilizing resources and soliciting the help of others who do know (for efficiency). You never need to know everything, but you absolutely have to be resourceful. Your service teaches kids how to be resourceful, by first identifying their need and utilizing your service as a resource, and secondly by going outside their comfort zone to follow your advice (which may mean more reaching out to others). You're teaching them how to be resourceful. That's probably why some kids don't like to work with you; they want you to just get them the job, not advise them on being resourceful."

This *New York Times* article[99] featured several entities trying to help students transition from college to the work world. Reading both the article and the comments section, I was taken by the negative views many folks had with the very concept of early career counseling. (Reading comments on the Internet often reminds me of rubbernecking; you get aggravated that you did it, but yet you do it again the next time.)

The article touched on some of the themes I wrote about in the Introduction of the book. Students have more choices, and a "furiously evolving career landscape," giving many "reason to fret." "'They face an entirely different reality than their parents did,' said Anthony P. Carnevale, director of the Georgetown University Center on Education and the Workforce."[100]

In the comments section, Emily Porschitz of LaunchingU (which does career coaching for college students and recent graduates) asserted, "Young adults ... are facing a brutally tough economy that they did not create, and levels of income inequality that previous generations could not have imagined. Mocking millennials for asking for support during one of life's major transitions is deplorable. College-to-career coaching is not an extension of an overindulged childhood, but rather another outgrowth of the coaching industry that so many of us use to navigate complicated transitions or major life challenges. Young adults need our support, not condescension."

As would be expected, I agree with Emily. Still, it's useful to take into account the thoughts of those who disagree. Below are some of the reactions I gleaned both from the article as well as from the commentary afterwards. Though I have an obvious bias, I've tried to analyze these theories, rather than to merely condemn them. Either way, this book wouldn't be finished without some examination of the coaching/mentoring process.

Asking for Help Makes You Strong, Not Weak

Comment: An incredibly measured, thoughtful comment came from a reader in Marin County, "'We have created a generation that doesn't want to make a mistake or fail.' That's all you need to read in this article. And it's sad. It takes many 'mistakes' or 'failures' for most people to find their groove — why do parents believe they can (or even should) control that? Why can't parents say they believe in their kids and they

---

99 https://www.nytimes.com/2016/04/10/education/edlife/career-coaching-for-the-playdate-generation.html?hp&action=click&pgtype=Homepage&clickSource=story-heading&module=mini-moth&region=top-stories-below&WT.nav=top-stories-below&_r=0

100 https://cew.georgetown.edu/

will support them in their dreams, and then leave it at that? If the kids aren't making 'bad' choices, why not let them figure it out for themselves? If it's out of fear that they won't find success, well, it's time we reexamine what 'success' means. There's enough research out there that speaks to what matters in the long run than our short-sighted view of 'success.' We should probably let our kids figure that out for themselves."

My Thoughts: One outgrowth about being scared of failure is that it leads to defeatism, or not trying, to avoid the rejection that accompanies failing. As a parent, accepting defeatism in your kid is extremely difficult. Clearly this writer is suggesting that by encouraging kids to try, even if they might fail, is itself a success. And that's very true. But I wonder whether there's more to this issue. For example, most students have a really hard time asking for help. Sure, there will always be those kids who approach professors to ask what material will be covered on the upcoming test. This isn't really asking for help; rather, it's trying to game a system and ensure a good result (a high grade). Compare this to what happens when professors say they are doing a group study session, and two kids out of 25 show up. Why is that? I posit that asking for help takes maturity. It can be embarrassing to admit you don't know something, or understand the class readings. Most students really struggle with this, and would rather "figure it out" on their own. Sure, that sounds admirable, but is it? Clearly, a balance exists between always asking for help first versus trying to learn on your own first. But limiting yourself to one or the other doesn't make you strong. When you've done all you can on your own, and when an expert is offering to guide you, take the help.

Beyond merely being able to overcome the hurdles asking for assistance presents, learning how to ask for guidance properly takes practice. What's more, implementing guidance takes nerve. It's easier to do things the way you've always done them (even if that method produces so-so outcomes). Changing your study methods, for example, might seem daunting. But if someone explains that doing so will markedly improve your grades, staying the same should no longer be an option.

As the previously referenced Maddie Thornburn, a wonderful Georgetown student with whom I worked, remarked, "It is important for young adults to understand it is okay to ask for help or guidance even though they are learning to be more independent. Asking for help is not a sign of weakness ... rather ... it shows preemptive recognition of uncertainty and /or failure. If you [the mentor] emphasize that you assist only when the student reaches out, it would show parents that their children must be proactive and take initiative, as they must learn to do so throughout the rest of their lives."

Indeed.

I Walked Five Miles to School, Uphill, Both Ways

Comment: "This is the 'I need a consultant for everything' generation - from SAT prep, to writing college essays, to discovering one's career. Pathetic - figure something out on your own for once."

My Thoughts: For the sake of argument, let's agree that those of us who grew up in the 1970s and 1980's had a different experience than kids do today, with less frills, less support, and less parental oversight. To that, I say, so what? My parents, in turn, would have argued (correctly) that THEIR growing up experience was significantly harder than mine was. My father was an orphan at 10. He was raised by older siblings, one of whom took him on her honeymoon because there was no one to take care of him otherwise. He never finished HS (I think a GED happened at some point). He somehow managed to go overseas at the tail end of WWII at age 16. 16. So yes, his early difficulties trumped mine, in a landslide. Did that mean he wanted me to repeat his experience? Not a chance. His main goal in life was for me to NOT have the life he'd had. His second goal was for me to figure out what I wanted to do, and then go do it. Whatever I had to do to make that happen, he encouraged. His lack of involvement in my decisions didn't stem solely, or even primarily, from some theory that this was best for me; rather, he was simply too busy working to know much about my school experiences (given the familiarity I had with the principal and detention, this worked in my favor). But when the time came to figure stuff out that I couldn't (or wouldn't) do on my own (like Financial Aid), you better believe he was there.

Now as a parent, I completely understand the above comment that today's generation "needs a consultant for everything." And in the next section, I'll discuss my thoughts on whether this makes kids over-coached, and if so, how they can get effectively coached instead. For now, let's agree that saying over-coaching demonstrates that today's kids are weak is not productive. For anyone.

Kids Today are Over-Coached

Article: Julie Olson-Buchanan, one of two professors of management who conducted a 2014 survey[101] of 482 students at California State University, Fresno, "found that those with the most intense helicopter parenting .... gave 'maladaptive responses' to workplace scenarios." For example, "When asked how they would respond to a nega-

---

101 http://www.emeraldinsight.com/doi/full/10.1108/ET-10-2012-0096

tive review from an employer, instead of focusing on how they might improve, they were more likely than peers to say they would quit, argue that the rating was unfair or ask a parent to call their manager."

My Thoughts: Yep, this is awful. It also has nothing to do with good coaching. Conflating helicopter parenting with effective coaching is not helping anyone. I'll let my first informal mentee and now head of my former company (and an incredible friend), Casey Drucker, take this one. After I sent her the article, Casey averred, "I … have strong feelings about the 'helicopter parenting' comments here. I disagree with the implication that hiring a coach for your kid is helicopter parenting. Actually, helicopter parenting is the opposite, i.e. not letting your kid be advised by someone who knows what they're doing so you remain the only one in control. Or, worse …hiring the coach/mentor and then interfering."

My young friend John Goodwin had more mixed feelings about this. I've presented his thoughts pretty much as is, given that trying to re-write his material is a fool's errand. John asked, "Is the focus on coaching a new requirement in the new, complex world faced by current grads, or just a continuation of the over-parenting that got them in the situation in the first place? Put another way, is this the antidote or more poison?"

Answering his own questions, John stated, "I imagine, as with most big questions, there are elements of truth on both sides. It sounds as if many of the subjects here are suffering from over-mommying, over-thinking, and a lack of cold hard responsibility. That said, however, I would acknowledge that (1) many of the things lacking are trained skills, so you need trainers, and (2) I am willing to at least entertain that today's job market/competition/etc. are qualitatively different in some aspects than they have been in the past. …"

Analyzing this further, John described it thusly: "Problem: yeah, maybe you did baby your kids too much.

Wrong fix: babying them more, OR just setting them adrift unprepared.

Right fix: teach them now to take responsibility and action in their life. No, they don't need to sit in a meditation circle and deeply evaluate their earliest memories to find out that they secretly want to be a physical therapist to circus animals. But they do need to (a) identify the salient factors in a career/lifestyle that will meaningfully impact their future happiness, and (b) Develop the tools and skills — networking, work ethic, etc. — that will enable them to identify and pursue opportunities in support of those factors."

College is the biggest transition kids will make ... until they leave, when they'll make the actual biggest transition of their lives. Learning who to ask for help, learning how to ask for help, and learning to integrate that help into action are skills that benefit all of us. College students are no exception.

An apt metaphor was sent to me by my close friend Arnie Herz: Students are often ill-prepared to transition from college to the real world. A bridge is needed; the mentor is the bridge.

Do College Kids Really Need More "Hand-Holding"?

Comment: "I spent time and effort modeling adult behavior so my three millennials could be self- sufficient, contributing members of society. Talk about a First World or a 1% problem? Eek."

My Thoughts: Naturally it would be better if kids simply developed grit on their own. It would be wonderful if they knew what they wanted. And it would be magnificent if the job market weren't so broad and so competitive. But that's fantasy land. We need to deal with the reality that exists.

Similar to the over-coached idea, the commenter's notion of self-sufficiency seems to tell only part of the story. (This book doesn't address the very valid First World issue raised in this comment. I'll leave that for a later book.) Of course every parent of a millennial is striving to have their children become self-sufficient. Of course modeling behavior that will lead to this is fantastic. But does this really mean that an 18 year-old should never ask anyone for anything? Is that being self-sufficient? And if they do ask for help, is helping them "holding their hand," with all the negative connotations associated with that juvenile phrase?

Many books describe how the young adult brain is in the most rapidly formative state that it will ever be in and is constantly forming habits and opinions. Most people experience improvement in performance and cognition through the use of specialists. From the dissemination of skills and information to bouncing ideas off of someone with relevant experience; from providing encouragement and examples to leveraging a network of connections in a given professional's field, the benefits are enormous.

Considering support systems and specialists to be "coddlers" is like thinking seeing a therapist for a mental issue or seeking a tutor to learn a subject are coddling. The least efficient way of learning things is to simply do everything on your own. This is not to be confused with having others do things for you. That is helicoptering at its worst.

Let's think of this in terms of networking. Helicoptering is contacting your friend, who then presents your kid an internship. In contrast, mentoring is explaining that forming deep relationships with people, based on actually giving a shit about what they say, is real networking. This is real life advice every kid can use. No one is holding their hand as they actually go out and execute the advice. That's the difference.

A brilliantly blunt psychologist I know explained that parenting in general is in a "weird cycle." We've gone from tough/do it on your own to protection/nurturing self-esteem. The products of that self-esteem generation are not faring well, and in many cases are floundering. Now a huge backlash is occurring. Regardless, she asserted, "this doesn't mean there's no role for coaching."

Get a Job ....But It Better Be an Internship with a Name-Brand Company

Comment: "I'm a GenX marketing director for a large tech company, and I'm an entrepreneur, author, and speaker. With or without paid coaches, Millennials need to bring a strong skill set to the party. Without that, nothing else matters. They need to communicate clearly about those skills when looking for a job. Also, Millennials are better served the sooner they learn how to network 'in the real world' and develop high-value relationships with people who can help them. Finally, they need mentors to guide them and monitor their progress. In other words, start hustling for yourself and don't depend on someone to make things happen for you."

My Thoughts: If you read this far, you know I have nothing to quibble about with this comment. The writer suggests a combination of doing for yourself with seeking guidance. So why even bring up this comment?

In my experience, lots of kids are receiving confusing, mixed messages from both their parents and their school career centers. Let's assume that parents and career centers have kids/students best interests in mind. So what's happening? Fear. Lack of safety and security that comes with a guaranteed job after graduation scares parents and colleges alike. Parents, because the idea of spending a fortune on a college student only to see him work at Starbucks after graduation, is terrifying. Colleges, because the percentage of students getting jobs within six months of leaving school is in jeopardy if students are unemployed; this number matters more and more in recruitment efforts.

Strong skill sets, with an emphasis on skills that can be transferred to multiple jobs and career paths, can be developed on ANY job a student holds. Not just one with a fancy branded internship. In fact, I'd argue that a fair amount of the latter positions do less for kids than the so-called scut job will. Lack of early work experience - whether it's sweeping the parking lot at the movie theater, babysitting or clerical work - is hugely problematic. Our biggest risk at my former company when hiring really young people always resulted from missing signs that a recent graduate had a silver-spoon-mentality (something that often came from lack of job experience).

My saucy college friend Tara put it like this: "With more career fields, doesn't that mean more opportunity? Seems like it would be easier to get a job albeit more difficult to narrow it down to what you may like. Failure is not always a bad thing. That's why kids should get summer jobs or part-time work during school to see what it means to work, be responsible and deal with adults as well as see what they like/don't like about each gig. Then they continue with internships. Duh."

Love Tara, and love the duh.

Coaching is Contrived

Comment: "It's best for kids to fail and rise on their own, especially these children with safety nets built of tangled parental hands. This why you should to start the 'what should I do with my life' process much earlier. .... The child won't need coaching for interviews or college essays, when the time comes, because: genuine résumé and genuine understanding and genuine voice and genuine direction and genuine character and genuine ambition.

Genuine beats contrived every time."

My Thoughts: No question – genuine beats contrived every time. All of the genuine items outlined in this comment are goals. Accomplishing those goals is the trick; with proper guidance, every student can figure out their genuine direction. Going it alone doesn't make the result more genuine. And the staggering number of under-employed graduates seems to indicate that going it alone also just doesn't work for many people. Mentoring that is worthwhile accelerates a student's process of finding himself and prevents lifelong under-employment.[102] Still, it is incumbent upon the student to find his way; the mentor helps outline the map, but can't take the actual steps.

---

102 http://creativemarbles.com/2015/06/27/welcome-to-the-new-adulthood/

Work is Work, and Jobs are Easy to Get

Comment: "Dear Playdate Generation,

It has always been the case (since colleges became open to all) that a lot of people, upon graduation, don't exactly know what they want to do with their lives. The way you find out is get a job or internship and Just Do It for about a year or two. If you turn out not to like it, you get another job. Rinse, repeat.

Unless you know already what you want to do, you are very likely to stumble onto what you really like by accident. It's ok. Success at your very first job looks like: 1. getting the job in the first place 2. being open enough and diligent enough to pass your probation and get along with co-workers 3. knowing, after the first year, if this job is for you or not.

Do not expect rainbows and unicorns. Work, all work, even in my job which is the best ever, is tedious, frustrating, boring. The trick is to find a place that in addition to all that, makes you happy in some, or many ways.

But hey, if you have $5K to spend on it, I can elaborate. In fact, I would be happy to..."

My Thoughts: This is some bitter sauce. We spend our lives in careers that many of us stumble into. Various estimates place the number of people who feel content with the careers they stumbled into at between 20% and 40%; these numbers don't even take into account the years and career switches required to get to the contented period. Why not make more deliberate decisions when thinking about the thing we're going to be spending the bulk of our time doing? As an employer, I'd much rather have the kid who really wants to work for me (or at least thinks he does). The kid who stumbles in? Pass.

As an aside, pointing out that work isn't all rainbows and unicorns is a little condescending. Sure, maybe some entitled kids do seem to believe that work is supposed to be fun. But the vast majority of students with whom I've come into contact are keenly aware that work can be tedious. There's a vast chasm between doing some tasks one finds boring and taking a job knowing all of the tasks will bore you.

The other thing this comment ignores is that people who have no enthusiasm or excitement for their work generally fail at that work. Most businesses can no longer afford loyalty; they say good bye to mediocre employees (and sometimes to good ones, but that's for another book). You will not have a long time to learn and even less time to show a willingness to learn. All B.S. is stripped away once money is on the line; people might at times get jobs because of some spurious family connection, but generally you won't keep one owing solely to this.

Colleges Do This For Free

Comment: "....There are many highly skilled people working in university career centers who provide almost exactly the same career assistance to students for free. The main difference is, college career advisors don't usually have the time to call every student every week to check up on them and make sure they did their homework. If a student can't be proactive enough to implement basic career advice regarding updating their résumé or applying to a job, how will they fare in an actual job, where their boss will not micromanage their every task?"

My Thoughts: This sounds so logical, so reasonable, that no one could argue with it. Except for one teensy thing: it's not true. Checking up with someone to see if they did their "homework" isn't a bad thing; doing someone's homework for them is. I have calls with mentees every two weeks. We review what they've been doing, and what they need to do before the next call. Micromanagement is overseeing every aspect of a student's life, which is impossible, even if one wanted to do it. Pushing a student to do things beyond which they thought possible is life-changing. And while it's not a college counselor's fault that he doesn't have time to get to know 500-2000 students, it's not OK to say you do everything a student needs in terms of guidance when the numbers prevent it. (One university in the article seems to be congratulating itself for now having 10 counselors – for 13,000 students.)

Courage Is Doing The Right Thing Even If You Look Silly.

My friend and Binghamton's newest real estate mogul (at the ripe age of 24), Adam Ibrahim (you might remember him from Chapter 11), pointed out something I'm hoping all you college students learn: do not let fear get in the way of listening, learning and changing. I get that it's easier to stay the same, even if doing so is ineffective, because making mistakes is "embarrassing." But college is all about making mistakes (and I don't just mean eating that 5th slice of sausage pizza at 3 am).

Why is it OK to make mistakes in college? Absent huge, obviously terrible long-lasting decisions, most of the "mistakes" you make, like saying the wrong answer in class, failing a test, taking a course you end up hating, trying a club that turns out to be dull, and making friends that you move away from the next semester, aren't really mistakes. All of these experiences move you on your path (cue the new age music here). So don't be afraid to try anything and everything your school offers. You'll be glad you did.

Listening to Malcolm Gladwell talk about Wilt Chamberlain, I was reminded of Wilt's famous statement regarding his notoriously poor free throw shooting. Wilt said he knew he'd been wrong not to continue shooting underhanded, which he'd done, successfully, for one season. He stopped because he felt he looked "silly."

A famous sociologist, Mark Granovetter, described this as high threshold behavior. He contrasted this with low threshold behavior, or doing the right thing regardless of what others think.

Guess which allows you to fulfill your potential? Wilt Chamberlain arguably should have been unstoppable. As it was he was amazing; still, his teams routinely TOOK HIM OUT OF THE GAME at the end because the other team simply fouled him, knowing they couldn't stop him but also knowing he shot free throws like someone who'd never played before.

Be the person who doesn't care so much about looking silly. Be unstoppable.

Speak Up

This past winter, in the midst of digging out my home from two and a half feet of snow, I was approached by my neighbor's 14 year-old son, who managed to ask me, in a very low voice, if I wanted him to pave my excruciatingly steep driveway. Immediately I said yes, and after negotiating a perfectly reasonable fee, I went inside to enjoy myself, with the only loser being my chiropractor.

While shoveling, I wasn't focused on my neighbor. Instead, he had to muster the courage to engage in business with me. We each emerged very satisfied, but just as easily could have found ourselves miserable, him with empty pockets, and me with a crooked spine.

Speak up. It works.

Final Homework Assignment:

Invest in yourself. Your future "you" is still …. you:

a. Take classes that challenge you. DON'T HIDE.
b. Take classes that interest you – even if you're not sure if or how they might help with your career path.

c. Take classes where you have to write.

d. Take classes forcing you to engage in some form of public speaking.

e. Join clubs – not just a frat/sorority.

f. Interact with kids who are not like you – geographically, economically, etc. – learn how to deal with them.

g. Meet your professors. Really meet them and establish relationships when you can.

h. Lead. In class, in clubs, everywhere. Just try it.

i. Identify a problem in your school or your neighborhood, and strive to fix it.

j. Get a job – any job. It doesn't always have to be a professional internship to be meaningful.

k. Learn to learn – employers will need you to think for yourself, not just do a task they assign to you.

l. Find, then foster, your passions.

m. Go deep with your skills.

n. Study what those skills and passions translate to, professionally.

o. Serendipity isn't random.[103] Cultivate your own.

p. Overcome your fears of not getting a job by preparing. Prepare by taking the above steps. Then be confident that it's worked.

q. Make yourself employable. Stand out from everyone else.

r. A résumé is just paper that gets you an interview. It's two dimensional. Your confidence and passion will get you a job. These things are three dimensional (hat tip to Nada Eldaif).

And finally, always remember that getting into college is great. Getting the most out of it is crucial. tm

---

103 https://www.nytimes.com/2016/01/03/opinion/how-to-cultivate-the-art-of-serendipity.html?_r=0

42059205R00103

Made in the USA
Middletown, DE
31 March 2017